Lit Crit

THE AWAKENING
OF ALBION

THE AWAKENING
OF ALBION

The Renovation of the Body in the Poetry of William Blake

by THOMAS R. FROSCH

Cornell University Press

ITHACA AND LONDON

First published 1974 by Cornell University Press.
Published in the United Kingdom by Cornell University Press Ltd., 2-4 Brook Street, London W1Y 1AA.

International Standard Book Number 0-8014-0815-6
Library of Congress Catalog Card Number 73-14063

Printed in the United States of America by Vail-Ballou Press, Inc.

FOR MY PARENTS,

John and Annette Frosch

Contents

Preface

Albion is Blake's Dreamer, akin to the great sleepers of
Joyce and Freud, and Blake's chief purpose as a poet was to
foresee his arising from "the nightmare of history." This
book is a study of Albion's resumption of consciousness and
of Blake's participation in the Romantic spirit of a complete
human renewal, a spirit, fundamentally secular, that asserted
the possibility of man's imaginative primacy over his conditions and that extended its vision beyond ideas of reform to
the prospect of society's re-entry into the Golden Age. *The
Awakening of Albion* is specifically a study of what seems to
be a pivotal phase of this spirit, the conviction that the transformation of man needed to include what can be described as
a resurrection of his body through a remaking of its sensory
organization.

With the later English Romantics, Blake learned enthusias-
tically from the Age of Revolution that the merely acquired
was not an inevitable destiny and that new beginnings were
possible. His eventual acknowledgment that the French Revolution had betrayed its original impulse by coming full
circle from monarchy to empire led not to any disillusion-
ment with social change but to an increasing insistence on
the deep conditions of authentic renovation. Societal despotism—political, religious, and moral—appeared to him

grounded in the individual in a tyranny of the ego, or self-hood, and of the reasoning mind at the expense of human wholeness, and these in turn appeared rooted in the bodily and perceptual particularities of our ordinary experience, and especially in a despotism of the eye.

The following essay is at odds, then, with any notion of a post-Revolutionary shift in Blake toward the purely personal or the transcendent. E. D. Hirsch, for instance, has written persuasively that Blake's work in the early 1790s represents a revolutionary naturalism, which is later repudiated in favor of a mystical and sacramental vision, the same one that is first explored in the *Songs of Innocence*.[1] Hirsch is correct in presenting Blake as a flexible poet, whose thinking and writing continually changed, but the changes are those of refinement, strengthening, and expansion, rather than recantation. My argument is that Blake's imagination was always conditioned by a drive toward the perceptual,[2] and that the complete description of the resurrected body given in Plates 96–99 of *Jerusalem* directly fulfills the radical impulses toward sensory renewal in *The Marriage of Heaven and Hell*.

The Awakening of Albion thus contributes to a concept in Blake studies, developed especially in the work of Northrop Frye, Peter Fisher, and Harold Bloom, that the Blakean renovation is at once visionary and anti-mystical.[3] Since the material that I am dealing with is difficult, it may be useful to set forth in advance the broad themes of the essay. In describing the way in which man's faculties are fragmented and eventually restored to an original interrelationship, my purpose is to show that renewal for Blake is not a transcendence but a reorganization of the given, that his critique of ordinary perception centers on an attack on perspectivism, that Blake conceives of the imagination as a perceptual, rather than purely mental, capacity, and that, ultimately, his proposal is for a metamorphosis of the senses through their engagement in the process of poetic work.

My approach is influenced, in a general way, by such phenomenologists as Gaston Bachelard and Maurice Merleau-Ponty and by the theories of perspective advanced by Marshall McLuhan; although I find Blake more extreme than the phenomenologists in refusing to acknowledge, as they tend to do, that the eye is "the axis of our world," [4] and sharply divergent from McLuhan, first, in maintaining a crucial distinction between the visual and the perspectival and, second, in studying the given body in the widest possible terms, not only as a product of technology but as the difficult, severely limited, and fallen condition of our experience. In discussions of Blakean vision major roles frequently have been assigned to Swedenborg and Boehme, but I have found nothing in their work so germane to the subject as Rilke's complaint that the modern poet is overpowered by the isolated sense of sight and his appeal that the world "be grasped by five levers at once"; [5] and I have tried to indicate, through occasional references, that the most useful points of analogy to Blake's myth of perception are to be seen in such writers as Wordsworth, Shelley, and Lawrence.

My aim is to bring together from the Blakean canon recurrent themes and images concerned with perception. To show that Blake's final presentation of the body is an amplification of his early views, I draw particularly from *Jerusalem* and the late work, where the topic has been least adequately observed. The sequence of chapters follows the overarching structure of Blake's myth from fall to redemption. Chapter 1 introduces to the general reader Blake's analysis of the problems of sensory experience and also surveys the chief critical approaches to the difficulties of that analysis. Chapter 2 considers Albion's original assumption of a physical being and the underlying conventions of his perceptual behavior. As the subject of Chapter 2 is the false creativity responsible for a fallen world, that of Chapter 3 is the authentic creativity capable of restoring paradise; and this unit focuses on the potentialities of renovation that exist within the world in the artist and in the natural senses. The final chapter studies the resurrection of the body in *The Four Zoas* and *Jerusalem* and the relationship of the last great awakening to three of the themes that preoccupied Blake's imagination: the role of art, the division of the sexes, and the primary quality of his universe, dialectical energy.

The most important of my general debts to other scholars are indicated above; in addition, I would like to note here my gratitude to Susan Fox, Morris Dickstein, and David N. Rollow, who read the manuscript of this book and were generous and acute with their suggestions, and, especially, to Harold Bloom, whose many kindnesses during my study of Blake it is a pleasure to acknowledge. I am also grateful to the Directors of the Arts and Science Research Fund of the Graduate School of New York University for a grant to provide assistance in the preparation of the manuscript.

Some of my material appeared in earlier form in my article "The New Body of English Romanticism" in *Soundings: An Interdisciplinary Journal* (Winter 1971).

THOMAS R. FROSCH

Queens College
of the City University
of New York

Textual Note

All quotations of Blake are from the unnormalized text edited by David V. Erdman, *The Poetry and Prose of William Blake,* commentary by Harold Bloom, 4th ed. (Garden City, N.Y.: Doubleday, 1970), copyright © 1965 by David Erdman and Harold Bloom, reprinted by permission of Doubleday & Company, Inc. I have added terminal punctuation to indented extracts but otherwise followed the spelling, punctuation, and capitalization of Erdman's text. References are given to the page number in this edition on which the cited passage begins (as E222). Plate or manuscript page and line numbers are given for the longer poems, and for *The Four Zoas, Milton,* and *Jerusalem* the number of the night, book, or chapter is included in Roman numeral (as F.Z. V: 65: 4–6, E337). In *The Four Zoas,* the revised and original versions of Night VII, as well as the first and second portions of divided manuscript pages, are designated as a and b. The Erdman pagination of *Jerusalem* differs from that of the Geoffrey Keynes text in the following plates: Erdman 29 is Keynes 33, 30–34, 31–35, 32–36, 33–37, 34–38, 35–39, 36–40, 37–41, 38–43, 39–44, 40–45, 41–46, 43–29, 44–30, 45–31, 46–32.

I use the following abbreviations for Blake's works:

A.   *America*

A.R.O.	*All Religions Are One*
B.T.	*The Book of Thel*
B.U.	*The Book of Urizen*
D.C.	*A Descriptive Catalogue*
E.	*Europe*
F.Z.	*The Four Zoas*
J.	*Jerusalem*
M.	*Milton*
M.H.H.	*The Marriage of Heaven and Hell*
N.N.R.	*There Is No Natural Religion*
S.E.	*Songs of Experience*
V.D.A.	*Visions of the Daughters of Albion*
V.L.J.	*A Vision of the Last Judgment*

Blake's marginal annotations to his readings are abbreviated as: Ann. to (name of author).

Quotations of Wordsworth, Shelley, and Keats are from the Oxford Standard Authors editions: *The Poetical Works of Wordsworth*, ed. Thomas Hutchinson, rev. Ernest de Selincourt (London, 1964); *The Poems of Shelley*, ed. Hutchinson (London, 1961); *The Poems of John Keats*, ed. H. W. Garrod (London, 1961).

THE AWAKENING
OF ALBION

CHAPTER 1

Caverned Man

> Five windows light the cavern'd Man; thro' one he breathes
>   the air;
> Thro' one, hears music of the spheres; thro' one, the eternal
>   vine
> Flourishes, that he may recieve the grapes; thro' one can
>   look.
> And see small portions of the eternal world that ever groweth;
> Thro' one, himself pass out what time he please, but he will
>   not;
> For stolen joys are sweet, & bread eaten in secret pleasant.
>   [E. iii: 1–6, E58]

In Blake's description of our fallen perception, the "real man" is a prisoner in the cavern of his skull or body or physical world as a whole. Taking in air and nourishment from without, he is a recipient of his own life, and such passivity characterizes his perception, as well. Product rather than producer, he is a *tabula rasa* inscribed by the light which enters through the five openings in the cavern, his five senses. Each sense hints of apocalyptic opportunity, and the fifth window offers complete liberation. This is the sense of touch, or sexuality, and it is also the power of execution, the body as an acting unit. But the possibility of an active body is refused, as the real man chooses the delights of an eroticized darkness, its enticing secrecy and its somehow pleasurable guilt.

The cognitive process of the caverned man is marked by the same passivity, as he reflects in the private sanctum of his mind upon the data that pass in from a world that is beyond his consciousness and incomprehensible in essence and extent. The word "reflection" and the other visual metaphors in the conventional description of our mentality are particularly suggestive here, for Blake takes the mind to be a larger, more powerful eye. Like the natural organ, the intellect focuses and isolates, separating experience into bits and pieces, even when its object is itself; and it completes its task by linking the fragments together in a picture, diagram, or pattern that is based on the eye's expectations but beyond its capacity. Knowledge, in this process, has ceased to be direct and immediate, far from a shock of vision that affects the complete man; rather, perception is split into a process of sensation and a process of synthesis. In *Prometheus Unbound,* Shelley's use of Panthea and Ione characterizes with great wit this division in our learning: whenever a new appearance enters the Titan's sensory field, one sister typically reports the novel impression while the other then attempts to explain or identify it. As long as the visionary capacity of Prometheus is imprisoned, it is only through this two-stage mediation that he can know.

When cognition is so pushed back from the act of perception, it necessarily operates in the mode of memory, as it works upon sensations which are past; and our habitual mental operations are further grounded in recollection insofar as we assimilate present sensations to past patterns of experience. For Wordsworth—even though he, like all the Romantics, was working for a style of immediate vision —memory is a way out, taking us back to a stage of development before the eye and intellect asserted their tyranny in us and thus opening a channel through which a new

perceptual energy can enter the body to reshape its possibilities. But for Blake any necessity of depending upon the
past in order to know is literally a living in the past and a
further refusal of the openings in the cavern. Not even such
knowledge as Coleridge's Ancient Mariner attains through
memories—an understanding that he is imprisoned by those
memories and by memory itself—is possible for Albion, who
gains no compensation for perpetually re-experiencing his
nightmare but, instead, slips deeper into sleep with each
recollection of his dilemma.

The problem goes back beyond misuse of our five senses
to the very existence of a five-sense body. Blake believes that
the human body changes, that it has a history, as rich and
specific as the history of thought. In particular, he takes the
given body to be an invention of the empiricism of Bacon
and Locke, whose "Philosophy of Five Senses" has deformed
us with a despotism of the visual by elevating the connection
between eye and mind to the status of a perceptual code of
law.[1] This theme is common to Romanticism, but Blake's
critique is particularly extreme, bringing him into conflict
with Wordsworth, as well as with the most important modern
critics of the given body, Rilke and D. H. Lawrence—all of
whom sought a humanistic paradise within the rhythms of
man's natural experience. For the empiricists and mechanists
of the eighteenth century, the primary condition of our
existence and our knowledge is that man is produced by
nature and educated by his experience of the natural world,
and this naturalism is to Blake the latest and most dangerous
in a series of human self-betrayals that goes back to the
nature-worship of the Celtic Druids and the matriarchal
mythologies of the Ancient Middle East. The figure of the
cavern refers to any assertion of man's passive dependence
upon nature, any concept of man as in essence a natural
being, and any qualification at all of the self-productive
capacity of consciousness.

This surrender to the given produces outside the cavern an autonomous environment, which we enter just as Adam enters the world of Genesis after it has been set up for him. Because it appears inexorably beyond our participation, it is characterized in its temporal aspect by the automatic recurrences of the natural cycle and by fate and destiny. Spatially it appears as a Mundane Shell, closed off by horizons and surrounded by void. There is thus such a thing as unfilled time, the time of clock and calendar, and unfilled space, or abyss, because time and space are pre-existent to us, what Merleau-Ponty would call "positive beings." This is a world of abstract pattern, and, although we feel completely dependent upon it, it can exist without us as a diagram on a sheet of paper. To Blake it is the Newtonian world, closed and predestined in that its development is organized by mechanical laws set in perpetual motion at its inception. Blake describes it as a monstrous contraption: "cruel Works / Of many Wheels I view, wheel without wheel, with cogs tyrannic / Moving by compulsion each other" (J. I: 15: 17–19, E157). Presiding over the machine is the God of convention, Blake's Urizen, guardian of the Decalogue. His name derived, apparently, from ὁρίζων, "separating circle, horizon," Urizen is a limit of expansion, an arbitrary *ne plus ultra* that bounds thought and perception and seeks to bound desire and imagination.

Unavailable to sense and attained only through reflection, the hidden deity governs a universe of awesome distances, for fallen experience is inevitably characterized by the remoteness of the objects of perception from the real man. Things have become secret and mysterious, and we are surrounded by unknown spaces—including the vague and unknown spaces of time, the past and future, including as well the remote and obscure spaces of other persons. The fading or disappearance of the other is always a leading motif in the Romantic crisis of consciousness; fallen lovers, as in

Prometheus Unbound, live in separate ravines. Like the persona in John Clare's "Secret Love," we can no longer find our loves, and Blake would agree with the later poet that this is because, chiefly in love with secrecy itself, we have hidden them. In the last line of the passage I have cited from *Europe,* Blake suggests that the sexualization of darkness and secrecy lies at the roots of fallen perception; and in a poem from his Notebook he ironically celebrates the efficacy of the arts of concealment in the achievement of desire:

> Never pain to tell thy love
> Love that never told can be
> For the gentle wind does move
> Silently invisibly
>
> I told my love I told my love
> I told her all my heart
> Trembling cold in ghastly fears
> Ah she doth depart
>
> Soon as she was gone from me
> A traveller came by
> Silently invisibly
> O was no deny.   [E458]

Alienation itself has become a sexual object. External nature is the remote, pedestaled mistress of a courtly ritual that extends far beyond its historical codification; the emotional phase of life, no less than the perceptual, mental, and religious, is given over to mysteries—or to Mystery, the Great Whore Rahab, who is Blake's fully revealed image of an idol nature. And the secrets of love and the secrets of God are caustically identified in "To Nobodaddy," from the Notebook:

> Why art thou silent & invisible
> Father of Jealousy
> Why dost thou hide thyself in clouds

> From every searching Eye
> Why darkness & obscurity
> In all thy words & laws
> That none dare eat the fruit but from
> The wily serpents jaws
> Or is it because Secrecy
> gains females loud applause?   [E462]

The "females" are, ultimately, all fallen humans, both lovers and mistresses in the courtly rites of the caverned world. Blake's man of reason is a cowering prisoner peeping out of the chinks or turning away from them into his own darkness, finally knowing nothing directly but a sense of obscurity and his own helplessness; the limits of his cavern, however, are sustained by his enjoyment of them, and his passiveness, his distances, his dependence on a world beyond his involvement, his sense of himself as imprisoned—all these are his dark pleasures.

But it is intrinsic to the caverned man's condition to have a sense of something more. The way things once were and the way they might again be, the opportunity of escape from the cavern—these are always with him. They are most powerfully with him as a frequent feeling of great energy in upsurge, energy often appearing as bodily and sexual, which runs against the limits and threatens to overwhelm them in seeking fulfillment. This titanic force Blake calls Orc, who is simultaneously the power of social revolution. What Lawrence has characterized as the "rebellion of life against convention," [2] Orc is the sense that the caverned form is not sufficient to our energy, that the Philosophy of Five Senses does not comprehend all that we feel we know, and that the limits are not *our* limits. That there is something more is also manifested as an awareness of what Blake calls other, "numerous" senses. Oothoon, in *Visions of the Daughters of Albion,* laments:

They told me that I had five senses to inclose me up.
And they inclos'd my infinite brain into a narrow circle.
And sunk my heart into the Abyss, a red round globe hot
    burning
Till all from life I was obliterated and erased.

[2: 31–34, E46]

Feeling that the limitation of our cognition to influxes
from the openings of sight, hearing, smell, taste, and touch
is merely arbitrary, she asks:

With what sense is it that the chicken shuns the ravenous
    hawk?
With what sense does the tame pigeon measure out the
    expanse?
With what sense does the bee form cells? have not the mouse
    & frog
Eyes and ears and sense of touch? yet are their habitations.
And their pursuits, as different as their forms and as their
    joys.   [3: 2–6]

Oothoon expresses the radical idea that each individuality
has its own valid perceptual possibilities; but her antagonist,
Bromion, invokes the "one law for both the lion and the
ox" to defend the concept of a standardized sensory system
and a consequently standardized world of valid appearances.
There are unknown things, because our five senses are weak;
they will be known when we mechanically empower our
senses, for the weak body needs aids to knowledge. But the
vision Oothoon speaks of is not to be found through devices
which merely strengthen and extend the given senses without
changing the structure of caverned perception: "The Micro-
scope knows not of this nor the Telescope. they alter / The
ratio of the Spectators Organs but leave Objects untouched"
(M. I: 29: 17–18, E126).

    In his early tractates against deism, Blake claims that the
organization of our faculties as a cavern with five windows is

geared toward our "eternal despair." Since what we can know according to this organization is less than what we can desire, fulfillment appears an impossibility. But Blake believes that the five senses are merely restrictions of our true faculties, which, although we have lost contact with them, are exactly sufficient to our desires: "He who sees the Infinite in all things sees God. He who sees the Ratio only sees himself only" (N.N.R. b, E2). And to see the "ratio," the mental aggregate of five-sense information, is to perceive nothing more than the form of one's dissatisfaction.

It is also to objectify one's own body. In five-sense perception the physical body is part of the external world and is itself known through its own windows. John Wild writes: "According to the naturalist, the human body is a physical object with definite boundaries, which is surrounded by other physical objects in geometric space. A physical object simply lies before us with its various properties as something there, *on hand,* to be gazed at from a detached point of view." [3] Man has a *soma,* or corpse, and is in his authentic being, a *psyche,* or life-shade.[4] The real man is liberated through the dissolution of his cavern, and D. H. Lawrence writes that all our religions since Socrates "have been religions of the dead body and the postponed reward." [5] When the body is thus considered to pertain to another dimension than that of consciousness, it is organized according to the principles of the external world: if the world is thought of as a machine, then so is the body. And the consequent relationship of body and self is given perhaps its most striking metaphor in *Lady Chatterley's Lover* in the anger and frustration that the paralyzed Clifford feels when he is unable to operate the levers of his motorized wheelchair.[6] Here the body, or faculty of motion, has become wholly a prosthetic extension of the man, and its powers are related to him as are those of a car or a telephone.

The loss of the body that affects so many other of Lawrence's characters, particularly his "intellectuals," can be understood in a Cartesian sense, as well as a Christian and a mechanistic, and the opening of the third *Meditation,* in which the body is chanted to sleep that the mind may come alive, is an exact illustration of Blake's image of the cavern: "Now I shall close my eyes, I shall stop my ears, I shall disregard my senses, I shall even efface from my mind all the images of corporeal things; or at least, since that can hardly be done, I shall consider them vain and false. By thus dealing only with myself and considering what is included in me, I shall try to make myself, little by little, better known and more familiar to myself." [7] But like all else, the prisoner can only be known to himself as a ratio; he is the "Human Abstract" (S.E., E27), the precipitation of our thoughts from our spaces, and the reductive idea of a full humanity, taken for the whole. The most acute contemporary student of this phenomenon is Samuel Beckett, whose Murphy, in trying to become pure mind, lulls his body with warmth and repose in his garret, only to achieve an unexpectedly complete self-abstraction when his stove explodes.

To Blake the body is the perceptible fragment of the soul. "Man has no Body distinct from his Soul for that calld Body is a portion of Soul discernd by the five Senses, the chief inlets of Soul in this age" (M.H.H.: 4, E34). The body is the effective circumference of imagination at any moment, and to regard its natural form as unchangeable is to give it the character of a cavern: "Lots Wife being Changed into Pillar of Salt alludes to the Mortal Body being rendered a Permanent Statue" (V.L.J.: 79, E546). For what Blake calls the "poetical genius" in every man to be actualized, the cavern of naturalistic perception must be renounced, in the same way, as Blake contends in "To Tirzah," that Jesus rejects the mother of his mortal part (S.E., E30). But Blake's concept of the resurrection must be clearly distinguished from that

understood by Pauline Christianity. The Body of Clay, which
is to be consumed, is the body as it is perceived naturalistically, and Blake is convinced that any program of mortifying
that body only sustains its existence, that, indeed, by mortifying the five inlets of the soul we diminish even more what
little of it we have left. Putting off mortality means to Blake
putting off the consciousness of the body as a natural object
in geometric space and of the faculties as five natural senses.

Blake is never willing in any way to renounce the here-and-
now, or to surrender his conviction that the body will be
risen in the world: "I feel that a Man may be happy in This
World. And I know that This World Is a World of Imagination & Vision I see Every thing I paint In This World, but
Every body does not see alike" (Letter to Dr. Trusler, Aug.
23, 1799, E676). The apocalypse he describes in *A Vision of
The Last Judgment* occurs in this life as an adjustment in
vision, a casting out of error and an embracing of truth; his
highest honorific is "humanity": "Thou art a Man God is
no more / Thy own humanity learn to adore" (E.G., E511).
And such a condition carries with it an ethic of responsibility
that is the counter to caverned apathy: "Why stand we here
trembling around / Calling on God for help; and not ourselves in whom God dwells" (J. II: 38: 12–13, E182).

Similarly, imagination for Blake does not exist beyond
form and matter, for desire without a distinct materialization
is synonymous with unfulfillment, and the energy that seeks
its liberation in specific acts becomes destructive and, in the
end, self-consuming, unless it finds them. This is the story
of "Ah! Sun-flower" (S.E., E25), in which the traveler, whose
vision cannot take him beyond a vague yearning, can only
look forward to the end of his seeking and desiring—or
death.

Our understanding of Blake, especially in his late work, is
still so encrusted with defining analogies to the impulses and
traditions of mysticism that it is necessary to emphasize that

for him imagination is a matter of perceptions and representations. Indeed, he suggests that forms of mental process
descend in validity as they forsake material particularity for
the opposite pole of mystery. The sensed phenomenon and its
abstraction are equally landscapes in which we live and act,
and to try to work apart from the images, like the mortifica-
tion of the body, is a retreat into the darkness of the cavern.

It follows that Blake is not interested in any God, paradise,
or fulfillment which is unavailable to the immediate experience of the body. The withdrawal from direct perception as a
trusted mode of cognition—the path carved out for us by
Plato, Paul, and Descartes—produces a fatal gap between
the real and the perceived, as does the empirical subordina-
tion of sensory detail to mental pattern; and when what we
take to be ultimate reality is removed from the world of appearances, so too is paradise, which is the state of our complete involvement in that reality. In *The Marriage of Heaven
and Hell,* Blake describes the retreat of the gods to the sky,
the disappearance of the sense of divine humanity from the
things around us, and our subsequent style of worshipping
realities that transcend our present experience (11, E37).
His suggestion is, further, that the distance between paradise
and our senses is simultaneous with that between involuntary
impression and conscious recognition. The cognition spoken
of in the following marginal comment to Berkeley's *Siris*
is a kind that, when it comes, bursts apart the world of our
customary experience: "Knowledge is not by deduction but
Immediate by Perception or Sense at once Christ addresses
himself to the Man not to his Reason" (E653). The feeling
in Blake, as in Wordsworth, Coleridge, Shelley, and Keats
after him, is that our present experience can be made whole
only by putting an end to the compartmentalization of our
awareness into unrelated, and often conflicting, modes of
knowing; and, like the later poets, Blake finds that for such
wholeness, a visionary knowledge and experience—one in

which the distance between the subject and the object disappears—must be sought through the body and the senses. Eden [8] will come about, Blake tells us, through "an improvement of sensual enjoyment" (M.H.H.: 14, E38).

In general terms, the freedom of the caverned man is "the liberty both of body & mind to exercise the Divine Arts of Imagination" (J. IV: 77, E229). The aim of this study is to explore the ramifications of that statement in Blake's poems and, specifically, to investigate the relationship, more complex than it may appear in this particular formulation, between "body" and "mind." It is in the description of this relationship that many of the most sophisticated discussions of the Blakean renovation tend to be least satisfactory.

In approaching the problem, Northrop Frye takes as his starting point Blake's difficult idea of seeing through and not with the eye. Frye writes: "We use five senses in perception, but if we used fifteen we should still have only a single mind. The eye does not see: the eye is a lens for the mind to look through. Perception, then, is not something we do with our senses; it is a mental act." And: "To be perceived, therefore, means to be imagined, to be related to an individual's pattern of experience, to become a part of his character." [9] This is inaccurate, because perception and synthesis remain two different things, and the imaginative work goes on behind the senses in an act of interpretation. Thus, when Frye notes, as he does repeatedly, that we must throw imagination and our whole being into the act of perception, he is saying something Blake might have approved, but not at all what Blake actually says in his most advanced formulations. By making of sense a lens, Frye both maintains the distinction between sense and imagination and makes it difficult to understand how the imagination could be liberated by an expansion of our perceptual organs. The body drops out of Frye's interpretation, and he becomes disturbingly figurative when he reads Blake on these matters, tending to make the poet tame and "sensible" when he is most highly unusual. When speaking of the expanded body of the reintegrated Albion, for instance, Frye becomes excessively allegorical, choosing to think of the expanded body as a visionary community of numerous men acting in unity or a body which has become larger in that it sees, imaginatively, more of life in relationship with itself, as if connected to it bodily, than it does now. Both these senses of Albion's risen body are very important, but there is also the quite literal sense of the risen body, which Frye does not convincingly take into account.[10]

Robert Gleckner, on the other hand, understands that Frye's formulation contradicts Blake's crucial principle that man has no body distinct from his soul.[11] He rejects Frye's antithesis of sight and vision and takes Blake literally when he speaks of our development, or our former possession, of larger and more numerous senses—not more eyes, Gleckner cautions, but more senses. Thus, the chinks in the cavern are multiplied and / or expanded until the cavern disappears and there is no longer a dichotomy of mental reality and perceptual appearance. By sticking closely in his thinking to a diagrammatic account of the cavern, trying to see how the body thus spatially represented can be opened up, Gleckner limits himself unnecessarily. Nor is he clear when he tries to reconcile the multiplying of our senses with what Blake tells us of the existence of four eternal senses in the risen man. And his article ends rather abruptly and cryptically by reminding us that all this is to be brought about by an improvement of sensual enjoyment.

Both Gleckner and Frye are on the right track in seeing that sense and imagination are ultimately bound up together. But, as the body and senses drop out of Frye's formulation, so the "liberty of the mind," the poetic imagination, has no place in Gleckner's. In neither account is the Blakean apocalypse convincingly described as a reorganization, rather than a transcendence, of the world. In neither, moreover, is it something truly of the body, for Gleckner, too, fails to keep the senses more than nominally within his formulation. In the end, he describes a spiritualized body in which the senses have been improved out of existence; like Hazard Adams in the following, he does not distinguish between "mind" and "imagination" and is thus snared by Blake into making a choice between the space inside the cavern and the space outside, attempting then to remake the whole according to one or the other: "The real world exists behind the eye, and the area behind the eye does not mirror the material world. The outer world is the activity of the mind projected in images." [12]

From the ways in which these formulations fall short, however, we can discern several guidelines for a further exploration of the problem. One is the essentially dynamic character of Blake's poetry. His poetic argumentation is always organized according to his myth of contraries: a progression through a conflict of opposites that affirm each other and in which neither term ever surrenders its particularity; a dialectic, then, like that of Lawrence, with his interest in dynamic polarity, and unlike that of Hegel, with his quest for synthesis. But it is important to understand that energy, more than a Blakean principle, is germane to all phases of his writing. He imagines in terms of process or activity, often turbulent, rather than in purely spatial "pictures," and the stationary is not only doctrinally inimical to him but poetically uncomfortable. To treat his formulations as static structures that can be represented in critical commentary by pictures or diagrams is a kind of reduction that runs counter to the fundamental qualities of his verse.[13] Indeed, the pictorial surface of an image is often exactly the object of his attack. His pivotal trope is that of motion stifled: a bird in a cage, the infant Orc in swaddling bands, man in his cavern. Incapable of adequate release, energy is deflected in the unsatisfying form of the voyage through space to "that sweet

golden clime / Where the travellers journey is done" ("Ah!
Sun-flower"); or it is discharged into pre-molded patterns of
an oppressive regularity, such as the natural cycle. But the
"solid without fluctuation" is the great illusion in Blake's
mythology, and no static or conventionally pictorial image
could suffice to describe the prisoner's emancipated state.

Second, Blake is fond of setting traps in which to catch our
habitual ways of thought, and one of these is the conflict he
presents between "spiritual" and "material." Although it
may seem that he is asking us to choose one or the other,
Blake feels that the conflict itself is false and that the option
is one between two errors of consciousness, the twin antip-
odes of the fall. Once a duality is established, to embrace
one pole and repudiate the other would merely intensify the
sense of fragmentation from which Blake is trying to free us.
Nor, again, can it be exactly true that the two terms are to be
taken as counters in a quasi-Hegelian dialectic, when both
thesis and antithesis are erroneous conceptions to begin with.
The Marriage shows that if we conceive of ourselves as un-
easy compounds of the angelic and the bestial, then by sub-
merging ourselves either in the angel or the beast we will
come to a kind of hell. Thus, the great monkeyhouse sequence (20, E41), Blake's commentary on the Yahoo-Houyhn-
hnm division, is both a parody of the way in which the
angels of orthodox religion and experimental philosophy devour the body, leaving a lifeless skeleton, and a parody, as
well, of the angel's secret fantasies of a bodily *dolce vita,* in
which, as it turns out, the liberty of the body looks more like
violence than love. Blake repudiates both asceticism and
mere sensualism, both the rejection and the total acceptance
of the natural body.[14]

It is on the question of dualism that Blake departs, perhaps
most crucially, from the properly mystical tradition. In Swedenborg, for example, each fallen human is composed of a
natural man, who perceives the external world, and an inner

man, who sees the external as a figure for the spiritual world. We are free to know according to one or the other, taking any object as letter or symbol, and consequently living our lives in either of two worlds. This kind of dualism inevitably takes the program of renovation out of the area of perception. When man has two sensory systems, renovation is no longer a sensory problem, for the real sphere of the redemptive drama is located between the two systems; it is a problem in choice, will, understanding, or allegiance.[15] Blake's anti-dualism is intimated in *The Marriage* in a fine transformation of an image from the Revelation of John. The beasts that rise from the sea and the earth and the harpers whose singing only the redeemed can hear are unified into a single figure, perceived as the terrifying Leviathan by the Swedenborgian angel and as a gentle singer by the "pitiable foolish young man" (Rev. 13–14; M.H.H.: 18–19, E40). There is only one world for Blake, and the given appearance of an object is a portion of its complete form, limited by the subject's capacity for vision. The final difficulty is not to choose, not even, precisely, to understand, but to see.

Together with Blake's commitment to energy and process, the irony with which he offers us fallacious choices, and his anti-dualistic concept of perceptual improvement, a final guideline is that when he speaks of a risen body, he means exactly that; David Erdman's point that *The Marriage of Heaven and Hell* "mocks those who can accept a spiritual apocalypse but are terrified at a resurrection of the body of society itself," [16] applies as well to the "body of man." And this is a resurrection, as the image of the cavern shows, that depends upon our fuller use of the faculties we have now. Blake, in a strikingly literal way, follows his acknowledged master, Ezekiel, in believing that "we have eyes to see, and see not . . . ears to hear, and hear not" (12:2).

CHAPTER 2

The Fallen World

Error

How did the caverned man come into being? Blake studied this question in a succession of poetic myths about the prisoner's original failure, what is called in *Jerusalem,* "Error." These myths have received numerous excellent descriptions, and my own commentary will be restricted chiefly to a single point. According to Hirsch, Blake's late concern with a visionary faculty of imagination stands in antithesis to his early concern with the natural senses; my suggestion in the following sketch of Blake's mythology of Error is that within his unique concept of perception both concerns are interrelated.

The primal story, given most fully in *The Four Zoas,* tells of the dismemberment of Albion, who is any man, mankind, England, and the world. He is the actual or potential human element in any situation, the perceiver, the consciousness, the body as subject; and it is Blake's belief that originally the entire universe consisted in Albion's integrated body and the creations of his desire. His fall takes the form of a compartmentalization of his body into the fundamental energies, or Zoas, that together, like a chariot, once bore his existence "from Eternity to Eternity." Now, in their fragmentation, these energies—Orc-Luvah (the emotional faculty and the sense of smell), Los-Urthona (the imagination and the sense of hearing), Urizen (the analytical intellect and the sense of sight), and Tharmas (the sense of touch and the body as a functioning unit)—go their separate ways as the clashing dimensions, categories, and ideologies of fallen history, as well as its emotional conflicts and its wars. When the Giant Forms renounce their participation in Albion's unity, the capability of each is reduced to his own selfhood, or spectre, and the cosmic man is left powerless, asleep on his rock, the geographical England, in the middle of the ocean. His faculties are now the controllers, rather than the vehicles, of his consciousness, and their self-interested activities serve only to reinforce his disintegration.

Blake associates each Zoa with a female form, or emanation, who embodies the achievement of his energy: Vala, the relationship of Luvah; Enitharmon, the creation of Los; Ahania, the comprehension of Urizen; and Enion, the act of Tharmas. In their unfallen integration, these four are the members of Jerusalem, the emanation of Albion's risen body, or his total liberty and fulfillment. But when the Zoas separate from Albion and from each other as spectres, the emanations fall away from Jerusalem to become what Blake calls shadows; and since one's emanation is the total form of otherness in one's life—one's spaces, loves, and acts—so the shadows express the character of fallen existence and represent not the success but the ultimate futility of the Zoas' particular efforts. Further, once the emanation is separated from the Zoa, she assumes a life and initiative of her own, gaining primacy over the spectre, who is suddenly confronted with an otherness completely independent of himself: the shadow of Jerusalem, or man's creative liberty, is Rahab-Babylon, or man's enslavement to nature.[1]

The topmost level of the story and the one that tends to receive central emphasis in the lyrical and narrative work prior to *The Four Zoas* analyzes the suppression of bodily energy by the Urizenic component in both society and the

self. In the fragmentation of the Zoas it is Urizen who attempts to steer Albion's total being. He is Reason self-ab-
sorbed, positing a higher world of pure thought, and casting
a judgment of doubt on everything that is not itself, and for
Blake, as for Wordsworth, the institution of an analytical
consciousness that subjects all forms of knowledge to its own
kind of questioning and demonstration, can only be the gen-
erator of new despair.[2] Urizen's critical authority operates
similarly as the dissector of our moral experience, as it ac-
cuses our senses and feelings of sin—that is, departure from
its own code—as well as inadequacy and error. The fallen
brain is Blake's Grand Inquisitor, and the spectral form of
Urizen in *The Four Zoas* is Satan, the infernal agency that
binds us by fear to the Sky God.

But Urizen's antagonist, Orc, the Messiah of sexual energy
and political revolution, cannot be contained; and his pe-
riodic upsurges, which include the birth of Jesus, reach their
culmination in a Second Coming, manifest in the political
upheavals of the eighteenth century. That the society threat-
ened by the French and American Revolutions is one
founded on sexual repression, Blake makes quite clear: "The
King & the Priest must be tied in a tether / Before two virgins can meet together" (E464). His early verse is rich in
Michelangelesque images of imprisonment and bondage;
and one complex of figures, relating to the trapping and
maltreatment of birds and animals, particularly conveys
Blake's sense of the dynamics of frustration, that "war is
energy Enslavd" (F.Z. IX: 120: 42, E375): "The Game Cock
clipd & armd for fight / Does the Rising Sun affright" ("Auguries of Innocence," E481). The animal energies of the body
will finally erupt in Orc, as he breaks the heavy chain "That
free Love with bondage bound" ("Earth's Answer," S.E.,
E19), and this liberation is the increase of sensual enjoyment
that will reconstitute the original titanic form of the body.
In defending against the demon of energy, the angels of po-

litical and religious reaction will attempt to "shut the five gates of their law-built heaven," or close the senses even more, but the fires of Orc "inwrap the earthly globe, yet man is not consumd" (A.: 16: 19, E56; 8: 15, E53).

But the body of Orc, although it remains in Blake's work to the end, is never taken as a way out by itself, not even in the early poems. Once we are disposed to use the faculties we have, once we are emotionally prepared for the celebration of sensory pleasure, new difficulties supervene. Like Shelley in "The Sensitive Plant," Blake believes that our organs are obscure and that love, beauty, and delight exceed their powers. We may use our senses with freedom and energy, but with the faculties we now have we can never discover forms that match our desire, or know directly what really exists for us. The constellations are Visions of Eternity, Blake writes in *Milton,* but we can see only "the hem of their garments . . . with our vegetable eyes" (see I: 25: 66–26:12, E121). And even in *The Marriage,* with its polemical appeals for instinctual freedom, Blake tells us that before our bodies can know the delights that are properly theirs, our senses must be cleansed so that these delights can be truly accommodated (14, E38). This does not indicate any suggestion in Blake that gratification must be postponed, but rather a feeling that Orc is only a necessary beginning and that his "ceaseless rage" for "the thrilling joys of sense" F. Z. V: 61: 17, E334) will only be satisfied in the terms of Albion's unfallen body.

Accordingly, in *The Four Zoas* emphasis is shifted to the total sense of fragmentation and loss of internal and external relationship that prevents any successful return of man's original energy. Blake's first epic tells on a mythic and historical plane the same story that the "crisis" poems of Words-worth and Coleridge do on an individual level, that of a crippling dejection and an inability to create, now in civilization itself. The crisis of Albion involves a rapid sequence of events, including Luvah's usurpation of the brain, the prov-

ince of Urizen, while the latter sleeps; the consequent warfare between mind and emotions; Tharmas' casting away of
his emanation in sexual shame and guilt; and a manifold
power struggle among the members of Albion, each acting
now out of jealousy and possessiveness. All of these situations
refer structurally to the phenomenon of individuation, a
powerful emergence of the sense of self in which the subject
is divided both from all else and within himself. This, the
Romantic crime, is the "sin" of the Ancient Mariner, who
in killing the albatross causes the world to retreat from him,
leaving him stranded and paralyzed; that of Prometheus, who
in giving authority to the reasoning mind raises Jupiter to
the sky as man's oppressor, and in effect chains himself to
the ravine; and that of Wordsworth, who in his acts of theft
in Book I of *The Prelude* implicitly recognizes a division
between himself and the world—what belongs to the ego and
what does not [3]—that will deepen until there is no interchange between the two: "*Caverns* there were within my
mind which sun / Could never penetrate" (III: 243-44). For
these poets, self-discovery is the fall of man, throwing him
back upon his "sole self"; and this detection, since it ac-
knowledges a separation of the subject from his world, is also
a discovery of death, a fall into mortality.[4]

The process of differentiation, once initiated, progresses
through an intensifying sequence of conflicts and estrange-
ments—the creation of the world we know, the unfolding of
western history—but, through its accumulation of seizures
and suppressions, it will eventually develop a counterforce
strong enough to overcome its destructiveness. Blake's problem as the poem advances is to define exactly what the counterforce is, and thus to define once again the specific failure
of the caverned man. What he arrives at, in a still tentative
and experimental way, is the centrality of Los, Albion's creative imagination. The decision is dictated by what was always the most radical of Blake's convictions. In *A Descrip-*

tive Catalogue and in the "Ancient Poets" passage of *The Marriage,* he tells us that the numerous senses of the poet once knew "visions of the eternal attributes, or divine names" (E527) in the things of nature: "Till a system was formed, which some took advantage of & enslav'd the vulgar by attempting to realize or abstract the mental deities from their objects; thus began Priesthood" (M.H.H.: 11, E37). The abstraction of the natural from the human erects the landscape as an autonomous being, and the one human body of Albion becomes the world of animal, vegetable, and mineral. "Tree & herb & fish & bird & beast [are] the scattered portions of his immortal body"; and his voice is heard "Screaming in birds over the deep & howling in the Wolf" (see F.Z. VIII: 110a: 1–28, E370). The concept of man's responsibility for his own percepts is thus embodied in a vision of the fall as a failure to sustain creative energy, a retreat from imagination, especially new imagination.

Accordingly, most of Blake's characters are depicted as workers and builders, and the actions of his narrative verse tend increasingly to be presented as types of productive labor until in *Jerusalem* an imagery of instruments and manufacture constitutes an almost continuous narrative matrix. The instrumental imagery of Los's forge—furnace, anvil, bellows, tongs, hammer—and of Enitharmon's weaving—loom, fiber, spindle, woof—figures most prominently in the poem, but Blake tells us of numerous other tools: the water-wheels of Newton; the instruments of binding and torture, such as the bands and the sacrificial knife; those of crucifixion, "Cross and Nails and Thorns and Spear"; and those of warfare: "swords; arrows; cannons; mortars / The terrible ball: the wedge: the loud sounding hammer of destruction" (III: 73: 11–12, E226). Similarly, the characters in the poem are constantly erecting buildings: "the Mills and Prisons and Workhouses of Og and Anak," "the feminine Tabernacle of Bacon, Newton, Locke," and Stonehenge, the Druidic city of rock,

Blake's Pandemonium: "Labour unparallelld! . . . a building of eternal death" (66: 6, 9, E216). Ultimately, every environment in the poem is a city built by the character who
lives there. Dominating the poem are Los's Golgonooza and
Enitharmon's "golden halls of Cathedron," the two cities
of imaginative and natural activity, and Jerusalem and Babylon, the two cities made by imagination and nature.

Jerusalem is concerned with the ultimate sources of our
experience, and the poem's great refrain, "Such are the Buildings of Los! and such are the Woofs of Enitharmon," referring to everything we know, drives home Blake's theme that
the primary creative forces of our world are men and women.
The appearances are man-made; all their changes are human
changes, even those natural and historical transmutations we
think of as wholly independent of us. Indeed, Blake's mytho-
poeic project, his "Bible of Hell," is a rewriting of history
that brings to the surface the connections between perceiver
and perceived, that reveals the development of natural and
social phenomena as a history of human vision and production. Blake's is an extreme statement of the position taken
by Rousseau ("We cannot touch, see, or hear, except as we
have been taught") [5] and, with negative implications, by Lawrence ("Men can only see according to a Convention").[6] Percepts, lives, and communities are artistic representations, and
all men are artists, good or bad; all forms are derived from
the Poetic Genius, and the body, like all else, is an imagin-
ing and a social contract at any historical moment. Blake's
characters, however, produce themselves and their world
with a purposeless fury, their creative programs driven by
a powerful impulse to organization, born of the loss of Albion's primal wholeness. Blakean man yearns for image and
body, for sense and form; this is perhaps his strongest instinct. That so many of his instruments are ultimately
weapons and that so many of his buildings and cities are
ultimately prisons reflects his deep failure. His efforts of

organization are invariably self-destructive, throwing the
creator back into the void or cavern from which his creation
was an attempted liberation.

Identifying our phenomena as poetic images and focusing
on a sickness in man's creative capacity, Blake thus places the
evolution of Los, the shaper of our perceptions, at the core of
his overarching narrative. In his first appearances in *The
Book of Urizen, The Book of Los,* and *The Four Zoas,* Los
is a Vulcan-like blacksmith, who takes over as demiurge when
Urizen, the self-proclaimed Supreme Being, fails to sustain a
rigid universe created out of pure mind. But what he does
in his frantic labor of internal and external compulsion is
to tie the fragments of Albion together in the most facile
possible structure, forging the links of fate, building the
skeleton, roofing over the fountain of thought. It is even Los
who binds the terrifying Orc to a rock as a sacrifice to Urizen,
an initial propitiation of the human to the natural that
firmly establishes Urizen's power as the tyrannical Sky God
and that, in addition, sets man's creative capacity at odds
with the energy from which it ultimately springs. As maker of
the fallen world, then, Los bears direct responsibility for its
conditions. At this point, the imagination is a servant of the
reasoning mind, forced to carry out the latter's furious search
for pattern, system, and code. The art of Los is one that ac-
cepts, rather than its own inspiration, the dominion of whatever ethos—religious, political, philosophical, or esthetic—
predominates in its environment; and such an art is described in *The Marriage* in the story of the debasement of
ancient mythopoesis into priestcraft: "Choosing forms of worship from poetic tales" (11, E37).

Los's making of the world, however, is a highly ambivalent
action, for, while it is a Urizenic codification, it also saves the
shattered fragments of eternity from total dissolution. Insofar
as he establishes the physical form of man and nature, as well
as the outlines of sight, his fallen structures are necessary to

prevent things from plunging further into an abyss of invisible abstractions: "But whatever is visible to the Generated Man, / Is a Creation of mercy & love, from the Satanic Void" (J. I: 44–45, E156). Now creating bodies not of the mind but of the senses, albeit of the natural eye, he thus can be said to be simultaneously rescuing and reducing perception. But his failure is to recognize the provisional quality of his inventions, and the visible limits needed to keep the world from chaos soon become idolized as absolute beings.

In the revised version of Night VII of *The Four Zoas,* Blake focuses on the healing of Los's crippled faculty. Here Los confronts his own selfhood, the Spectre of Urthona, who embodies all the forces within him that militate against his impulse toward a universal renovation; in the terms of Shelley's "Adonais," the Spectre is the weakness with which the Power is girt round.[7] He is the ratio of the given senses, the "Body of Doubt" that Los must struggle to surpass. But the natural body is all the poet has to work with, the limited capacity of the imagination to produce real results; and only by entering the five senses can the imagination expand them beyond their fallen limits. Thus the poetic faculty must work both with and against the given senses at the same time.

In *Milton,* Blake expands his analysis of the obstructions within the imagination. Blake's *Prelude* and his *Confessions,* the poem concerns the evolution of its author from bard to prophet, as he is joined to Milton, his poetic forerunner, and to Los, the Prophetic Spirit, who is the Power within both. Four primary failures are confronted in this adventure. The first is the resistance of the imagination to the mortality that is not native to it. Milton must be willing to return to the world; like Keats's Apollo in *Hyperion* he must "die into life" and accept an incarnation in a particular poet, a man speaking to men. Blake, like the other Romantics, has no interest in an ineffable imagination, completed within itself but transcending all else, for this would merely be another

form of estranged consciousness, one more secret in the
depths of the cavern. The second failure is the tendency in
even the greatest of poets to deny finally the autonomy of his
own imagination in favor of the fundamental assumptions
of his civilization; chiefly, Milton must learn to recognize
Satan not as God's demonic opposer but as his spectral inversion, as "the Mind of the Natural Frame" (Ann. to Bacon,
E615). The third is that the Satan, or "Reasoning Negative,"
in the poet can usurp and disorganize his talent. Thus Rintrah, Palamabron and Satan battle for predominance among
Los's workers. Rintrah and Palamabron coexist in the poet as
the fury of prophecy and the beauty and compassion of art.
In Blake's age, the poet is Palamabron, a bringer of pleasure
and empathy; but to be merely Palamabron in a spectral
world is to be a subtle perpetrator of Albion's nightmare, for
the dreams of Beulah, when regarded as permissible vaca-
tions from a fallen reality, serve only to reinforce what they
seem to oppose. Thus, Satan usurps Palamabron's place: or
in other words, Satan is the ultimate form of Palamabron
when the beauty of art is taken as an end in itself.

The fourth error of the imagination is its surrender to its
own shadow. In Book II, Milton's emanation, Ololon, must be
readied for a new marriage in the world, much as Shelley's
Asia must undergo a separate passage to prepare her for reunification with Prometheus. As Milton must descend from
Eden, the eternal home of the creative, so Ololon must accept
a descent from Beulah, the paradise of the created. Ololon's
preparation is, in one sense, the passage of Milton's creative
idea from inspiration, the subject of Book I, to actual poem:
the emanation must assent to a fallen and imperfect form,
and it must, as the canon of Milton's former work, renounce
its own completed status and open itself to correction, revision, and continuation. In addition, as the poet's love in the
world, Ololon must work her way out of the envy and arro-
gance, as well as a disdain of sexuality, with which the ema-

nations are affected when Albion's dismemberment casts
them loose and gives them a will-to-power of their own.
Blake's study of the relationship between the spectral poet
and his emanation is continued in *Jerusalem* in the struggle
of Los against Enitharmon, the weaver of natural bodies.
When genuine creativity is felt to belong not to man but to
nature, the poetic consciousness denies its own particularity
and retires into spectral modes of creation that draw on memory, experience, and sensation, rather than inspiration.
Throughout *Jerusalem* Los is shown both succumbing to
and struggling against "the sweet delights of secret amorous
glances" with which Enitharmon asserts the primacy of the
object-world:

> I know I am Urthona keeper of the Gates of Heaven,
> And that I can at will expatiate in the Gardens of bliss;
> But pangs of love draw me down to my loins which are
> Become a fountain of veiny pipes: O Albion! my brother!
>   [IV: 82: 81–84, E238]

In the final epic, then, Los must continue to resist the
temptations to self-betrayal offered by Enitharmon and the
Spectre of Urthona, and the assumption of the poetical character is portrayed as a constant process. But where the conception of *Jerusalem* breaks most extraordinarily into new
territory is in its giving epic treatment to the poetic process
itself. Blake's story now tells of the struggle of Los to write
a poem, of man's imagination to free itself from its natural
conditions, restore its own creative primacy in the world and
remake the appearances. Los's labor of increasing and altering perception through his art is pitted against the creative
efforts of all the other characters, or man's remaining faculties, whose products can be described as history, nature, and
civilization. Their labors of false creation are summarized in
Albion, who constantly relives and reconfirms his fall: forsaking Jerusalem for the idol Vala, repudiating an imaginative

for a natural life, surrendering to guilt, jealousy, and fear of sexual energy, resisting renewal under the guise of moralism, and deifying Satan, his own selfhood. As *Jerusalem*'s great image of renovative action is the human form of Los, laboring at his forge and constantly confronting the limits of his senses, Albion's sleeping body is the poem's dominant image of our submission to the given and our consequent antagonism to our own restoration; in Albion's viewpoint Los is the chief enemy.

Thus, in its final refinement Blake's mythology of Error centers on Albion's rejection of his own poetic faculty, his own numerous senses; his refusal includes within its scope the problems of sexual repression and individuation, for it represents a total repudiation of man's original divine body; and it is a rejection that manifests itself in the normative activity of his five natural senses. Blake's development reveals an increasing conviction that beyond the celebration of the body and the attack on unnecessary moral restrictions is a labor of uprooting the habitual structures of ordinary perception that keep man from his own energy; and it is to a more detailed consideration of these structures that we will now turn.

The Creation of the Body

The central product of Albion's creative failure is the human body itself. The motif of its forming is one on which Blake, as a narrative artist, rang many changes; but basic to all the treatments is a double theme: that the "creation" of man is an act of destruction, an attempt to annihilate his unfallen body and is thus portrayed as a torture or murder; and, at the same time, that the eternal body cannot be annihilated, but only deformed, suppressed, or forced into exile. Tharmas tells Urizen: "The Body of Man is given to me

I seek in vain to destroy / For still it surges forth in fish &
monsters of the deeps" (F.Z. VI: 69: 11–12, E339).

The most extensive description of the creation of the body
occurs in *The Four Zoas* in a passage taken with modifica-
tions, chiefly prosodic, from *The Book of Urizen*. Los begins
by englobing the "fountain of thought," and upon the base
of a caverned brain the rest of the body is established, for it
is a body of limits and horizons. It takes Seven Dismal Ages
for Los to complete the first natural body, that of Urizen, the
anthropomorphic God. In the First Age, he builds the skeleton:

> In a horrible dreamful slumber like the linked chain
> A vast spine writhd in torment upon the wind
> Shooting paind. ribbs like a bending Cavern
> And bones of solidness froze over all his nerves of joy.
>
> [IV: 54: 11–14, E330]

After making the brain, Los drops out of the description, for
once the fountain of thought is enclosed, the rest necessarily
forms itself according to the mechanics of its own first cause.
The Second Age evolves a globe-like natural heart and its
circulatory system, depicted as a web of entangling roots:

> From the Caverns of his jointed spine down sunk with fright
> A red round globe. hot burning. deep deep down into the
>   Abyss
> Panting Conglobing trembling Shooting out ten thousand
>   branches
> Around his solid bones & a Second Age passed over.   [16–19]

Next come the eyes, which fearfully react by englobing themselves and which behold depth and distance:

> In harrowing fear rolling his nervous brain shot branches
> On high into two little orbs hiding in two little caves
> Hiding carefully from the wind his eyes beheld the deep.
>
> [20–22]

The ears, notably, are born in hope, for, as we will see, they represent the way out of the fallen body. But now, before Los has attained his prophetic identity, the hope is all but obliterated in agony, and the ears themselves appear externalized and solidified:

> The pangs of hope began in heavy pain striving struggling
> Two Ears in close volutions from beneath his orbs of vision
> Shot spiring out & petrified as they grew.   [24–26]

The nostrils are turned to the ground of nature and to the emptiness of the Mundane space: "In ghastly torment sick hanging down upon the wind / Two nostrils bent down to the deeps" (28–29). Next is the digestive system with its hungering and thirsting tongue, for this is, quite literally throughout Blake's poetry, the body of the Devourer (see M.H.H. 16, E39); and, also, a body condemned by the circumstances that brought it about to be always yearning for a fulfillment it can never achieve in the natural terms of its operation:

> In ghastly torment sick. within his ribs bloated round
> A craving hungry cavern. Thence arose his channeld
> Throat. then like a red flame a tongue of hunger
> And thirst appeard and a sixth age passed of dismal woe.
>
>   [55: 2–5]

And finally the sense of touch, the limbs and the power of locomotion, the new body as an acting whole, which operates in the pure space of the void and, in its desperate transformation of tactility into possessiveness, actually touches nothing:

> Enraged & stifled with torment he threw his right arm to the
>   north
> His left arm to the south shooting out in anguish deep
> And his feet stampd the nether abyss in trembling howling &
>   dismay.   [6–8]

In other descriptions, the creation is a sundering or a tearing apart. In *Jerusalem* the Daughters of Albion, presiding geniuses of nature, are said to divide Luvah into the three dimensions of space, as well as into three obscure human regions: a transcendental, a subterranean, and a secretive, or head, loins, and heart. Simultaneously, Los gives a separate place to each faculty of Reuben, the ordinary fallen man, thus compartmentalizing the imagination into organs and into different classes of cognitive possibility (see II: 30: 43– 32: 24, E175). Tearing asunder is enumeration and categorization, a measuring of finite parts; so Tirzah in *Milton* "numbers with her fingers every fibre ere it grow" (I: 19: 49, E112), and, as the hag in "The Mental Traveller," "Her fingers number every Nerve / Just as a miser counts his gold" (E475).

Sometimes the body is depicted as forming itself in reaction to the new remoteness or hostility of its environment. In *The Book of Ahania,* Fuzon, the "pale living Corse" and an Orc figure, is nailed to the Tree of Mystery and takes a natural shape in reaction to the "arrows of pestilence" which assault him:

> The shapes screaming flutter'd vain
> Some combin'd into muscles & glands
> Some organs for craving and lust
> Most remain'd on the tormented void.   [4: 31–34, E87]

Man's expansiveness, newly susceptible to the ravages of organic matter, combines into a natural anatomy in response to an onslaught of disease.[8] And in *The Four Zoas* Urizen's body solidifies as he grasps after the "Shadowy Female"; as the emanation becomes misty and indefinite, the human becomes rock-like:

> His teeth a triple row he strove to sieze the shadow in vain
> And his immense tail lashd the Abyss his human form a
>   Stone

A form of Senseless Stone remaind in terrors on the rock.
[F.Z. VIII: 106b: 30–32, E367]

Creation is also a diminishment. Satan, in "The fields from Islington to Marybone," has withered up the Human Form into a mortal worm—elsewhere of sixty or seventy inches or winters, man's physical and chronological measure; and Jerusalem, seeking the original expansive forms of humanity, finds only "narrow places in a little and dark land," with Albion himself "shrunk to a narrow rock in the midst of the sea!" (J. IV: 79: 22–63, E232).

Concomitant with man's diminishment is an expansion of his environment, to the point that he appears to himself as a particle within a cosmic enormity, lost "In Chasms & Abysses of sorrow, enlarg'd without dimension, terrible" (J. I: 5: 5, E146). In the new world of terrifying size and distances the objects of direct perception are radically reduced, shrinking away both from man and from each other; and included among the objects that shrink from immediate knowledge is man's own body, for not only has the body assumed a place, to the mind's eye, among external things, but it has also gone "underground" in that its instincts and processes have passed beyond our senses, and all we can perceive of it is a slight surface, a skin over the raging, unknown waters of Tharmas: "The Lungs, the Heart, the Liver, shrunk away far distant from Man / And left a little slimy substance floating upon the tides" (J. II: 49: 17–18, E196). Such a body and such a world of objects are too small to sustain man's energy and love; recognizing that he lives in a world that can never satisfy him, Los perceives his emanation, or the possibility of his actual fulfillment, as withered almost to the point of a complete vanishing:

How art thou Shrunk thy grapes that burst in summers vast
    Excess
Shut up in little purple covering faintly bud & die

Thy olive trees that pourd down oil upon a thousand hills
Sickly look forth & scarcely stretch their branches to the
plain
Thy roses that expanded in the face of glowing morn

Hid in a little silken veil scarce breathe & faintly shine
Thy lilies that gave light what time the morning looked
forth
Hid in the Vales faintly lament & no one hears their voice.
[F.Z. VIIa: 81: 29–82: 3, E350]

Blake concentrates on such details as the muting of voices,
for the creation of the fallen body represents a drastic loss in
communication. Blakean characters have lost the capacity to
speak with each other almost as totally as they have lost the
capacity to speak with animals and trees, for their desperate
attempts at articulation produce only a welter of competing
private languages. The power in the fallen sense of giving
and receiving utterance has so diminished that it sometimes
seems as if man lives wholly in a world of nonsignificative
sound, or mere noise. Urizen, for instance, cannot speak to
his "ruined children," the lions, tigers, serpents, and other
monsters of fierce energy, who are "dishumanized men":
"His voice to them was but an inarticulate thunder for their
Ears / Were heavy & dull & their eyes & nostrils closed up"
(F.Z. VI: 70a: 39–40, E340). This is literally the thunder we
hear in the sky, the ominous, disembodied Word of the Sky
God. That language, Blake intimates, is only a function of
the dulled state of our senses. If our ears, eyes, and nostrils
were opened, there would be no thunder.

Blake is always bringing us home to the five senses and
their failures; for him, they are the measure of all our losses
and all our despair. The following lament in *Milton* is his
most extensive catalogue of their inadequacy:

Ah weak & wide astray! Ah shut in narrow doleful form
Creeping in reptile flesh upon the bosom of the ground

The Eye of Man a little narrow orb closd up & dark
Scarcely beholding the great light conversing with the Void
The Ear, a little shell in small volutions shutting out
All melodies & comprehending only Discord and Harmony
The Tongue a little moisture fills, a little food it cloys
A little sound it utters & its cries are faintly heard
Then brings forth Moral Virtue the cruel Virgin Babylon

Can such an Eye judge of the stars? & looking thro its tubes
Measure the sunny rays that point their spears on Udanadan
Can such an Ear filld with the vapours of the yawning pit.
Judge of the pure melodious harp struck by a hand divine?
Can such closed Nostrils feel a joy? or tell of autumn fruits
When grapes & figs burst their covering to the joyful air
Can such a Tongue boast of the living waters? or take in
Ought but the Vegetable Ratio & loathe the faint delight
Can such gross Lips percieve? alas! folded within themselves
They touch not ought but pallid turn & tremble at every
    wind.   [I: 5: 19–37, E98]

In a similar passage, Thel, with the curiosity of innocence,
poignantly wonders why there should be "a tender curb
upon the youthful burning boy! Why a little curtain of flesh
on the bed of our desires?" (E6). Her discovery of the mature
body yields a feeling, powerful enough to drive her emotionally back to childhood, that there is something "un-
natural" about the natural body, that its desire and its organization run counter to one another, that it is a form
geared to its own frustration. Yet, Blake says, even as we
lament the inadequacy of our natural bodies, we contrive to
wither them even more "by Laws of Sacrifice for Sin / By
Laws of Chastity & Abhorrence" (J. II: 49: 25–26, E196).

The sacrifice is specifically the binding of Orc and constitutes the second stage in the manufacture of our physical
being. The body of Orc is made of all that has been excluded
from Los's original construction, of all our memories and
anticipations of lost faculties, of our sheer craving for sensory

experience. When Blake describes Orc, he is matched in his portrayal of a fundamental human need for the things of the senses perhaps only by Keats, with the latter's poetic stance of straining on tiptoe to see, hear, touch, taste, and smell as much as possible. But in Blake the return of the body is a fiercer phenomenon, for it comes to claim its revenge on its dispossessors:

> ten thousand thousand spirits
> Of life lament around the Demon going forth & returning
> At his enormous call they flee into the heavens of heavens
> And back return with wine & food. Or dive into the deeps
> To bring the thrilling joys of sense to quell his ceaseless rage.

"Such is the Demon such his terror in the nether deep" (see F.Z. V: 61: 11–62: 8, E334). The exuberance of Orc's return is ironic, because he will not find enough in the fallen world to satisfy his need. Further, whenever the body of Orc appears, the energy that would consume the cycles of Generation is harnessed to propel them. Through the binding, and the torture that accompanies it, the Demon is given a natural form; our bodies are created for us anew with each sensory experience, and every expression of energy in natural terms repeats the original withering, or crucifixion, of Albion's Divine Body.

While the ceremony of binding is variously performed by Urizen, the witch Tirzah, or Orc's parents, Los and Enitharmon, its greatest image is that of the Druidic Sacrifice, most often carried out by the Daughters of Albion. In Blake, Druidism comprehends every full-scale program and every minute act which sacrifices the human to the natural; [9] finding divinity in the landscape, the Druids "began to turn allegoric and mental signification into corporeal command, whereby human sacrifice would have depopulated the earth" (D.C., E533). When we sever symbol and letter and take, as a holy first principle, the purely mental form, the deity as it is distinct from the human breast, we are committing a physical sacrifice, as the Druids killed their victims to assuage invisible naturalistic deities. Blake's fury, his sheer horror and anger at the spectacle of human suppression, is unmistakable in the details of his imagery. Things are separated from Albion by being literally sliced from his body with a knife; the body and senses of man, in a commonly repeated tag-line, shrink under the sacrificial knife, as man becomes a howling victim on an altar in the Oaken Groves, or Druidic Church of Vegetation. One of the most audacious of Blake's recurrent images, the sacrifice figures with particular frequency through *Jerusalem* and is given its definitive elaboration in a passage of almost 300 lines (III: 65, E214). It is instructive that Blake's strongest and dramatically most elaborate denunciation of sexual restriction occurs in the poem that is still often held to represent most clearly his turning away from the natural body.

The episode tells specifically of the original murder of Luvah; but, opening with the nailing of the Zoa to a tree, it also invokes the crucifixion of Jesus and, beyond that, any act in which revolutionary desire is naturalized and civilized. Present at the scene are the Sons and Daughters of Albion, society and nature, accomplices in the sacrifice of sexual energy. Placing their victim on the Decalogue-like Stone of Trial in the Oaken Groves, the delighted Daughters sport about him, like Bacchantes drinking his life "in sweet intoxication." As the victim's form is tortured into alteration, the Sons of Albion behold it with terror, but the response to their dread is to intensify the torment; they institutionalize their practice in the code of Natural Religion and construct Stonehenge, the rock city of sacrifice. The Daughters continue to build the natural body by surgically operating on the victim:

> They take off his vesture whole with their Knives of flint:
> But they cut asunder his inner garments: searching with

> Their cruel fingers for his heart, & there they enter in pomp,
> In many tears; & there they erect a temple & an altar:
> They pour cold water on his brain in front, to cause
> Lids to grow over his eyes in veils of tears: and caverns
> To freeze over his nostrils.   [66: 26–32, E216]

The Blakean irony is that there is no escape from the law of self-creation. All who see are similarly transformed: "As their Victim, so are they in the pangs / Of unconquerable fear!" (38–39).

Gradually the world of "indefinite cloudy shadows" comes into being, for as the victim's body is shaped, with each alteration there is necessarily a corresponding variation in his percepts. The blood that gushes from the victim stains all nature, and the rivers, like the Daughters, become "drunk with the blood of the slain." At the sight of this brutality, the objects of perception flee from the senses in fear: animals "generate in rocky places desolate / They return not; but build a habitation separate from Man"; "The Stars flee remote: the heaven is iron, the earth is sulphur / And all the mountains & hills shrink up like a withering gourd" (see 69–84, E217). The Daughters are now described as vampires drinking the victim's blood, and soon they become cannibals eating his roasted flesh. They weave a human form appropriate to their appetite:

> Ashamed to give Love openly to the piteous & merciful Man
> Counting him an imbecile mockery: but the Warrior
> They adore: & his revenge cherish with the blood of the
>   Innocent.   [67:19–21, E218]

Simultaneously, the world of departed percepts takes on a hostile character, both toward man and within itself:

> Loud the Sun & Moon rage in the conflict: loud the Stars
> Shout in the night of battle & their spears grow to their hands
> With blood, weaving the deaths of the Mighty into a Taber-
>   nacle

> For Rahab & Tirzah; till the Great Polypus of Generation
>   covered the Earth. [31–34]

The head of the Polypus, the formless devouring monster of
organic matter, is Verulam, home of the empiricist Bacon;
and the human brain is accommodated to the five-sense
system of natural reason by being "circumscribed beneath"
and pierced "thro the midst with a golden pin," giving it the
structure of a compass, the instrument with which Urizen
measures out his horizons in the painting "The Ancient of
Days." The feminine portion of the empirical brain of the
Polypus is Tirzah, the natural percept of the five-sense
system, the mother of our mortal part, and in this passage
she is directly identified as Rahab, Blake's Whore of Babylon. Pitying the "poor child of woe" she has made, she begs
the human form to turn to her in love. If it will not, she
threatens further torments: thus the inception of natural
love, as the sacrifice is subtly modulated into its sophisticated
format, the torments of love and jealousy: "If thou dost go
away from me I shall consume upon these Rocks":

> Go Noah fetch the girdle of strong brass, heat it red-hot:
> Press it around the loins of this ever expanding cruelty
> Shriek not so my only love! I refuse thy joys. [46, 59–61]

The motif develops further as the untouchable Daughters
of Albion "sport before the Kings," denying fulfillment of
the desire they arouse and stirring the taste for blood. They
spread like roots over the nations, demanding as sacrificial
offerings "your first begotten" (68: 30–37, E220). Energy,
directed toward sexual objects closed off by the codifica-
tions of denial and toward the forms of nature which are
not, in the first place, sufficient to a complete fulfillment, is
deflected into the same violent forms of expression which
brought it into its bound state. There, the ideal form of the
Daughters, the warrior—and the warrior in all men—finds
his pleasure, hoping through his own sacrificial work to win
his mistress:

                                    I am drunk with unsatiated love
I must rush again to War: for the Virgin has frownd & refusd
Sometimes I curse & sometimes bless thy fascinating beauty
Once Man was occupied in intellectual pleasures & energies
But now my soul is harrowd with grief & fear & love & desire
And now I hate & now I love & Intellect is no more:
There is no time for any thing but the torments of love &
    desire. [62–68]

The transformation of the Orc body is complete as it consumes its energy in programs of self-destruction, which reinforce the dominion of the emanation. The Satanic anthro-
pogeny is accomplished in the satisfactory body of selfhood,
the body of the warrior; and the beauty of human desire is
now successfully integrated into the spectral world.

The Dynamics of Fallen Perception

The initial shocks of the creation of the body and the
sacrifice of Orc-Luvah establish not only a world but also a
set of conventions through which we continue to perceive
and relate to our objects and our selves. Blake explores these
mechanisms of Error in several recurrent structures—externalization, expansion and contraction, the vortex, and the
center and circumference—figures that contain some of his
most difficult material. Kathleen Raine has recently analyzed
such Blakean structures in terms of occult and Neoplatonic
symbology; [10] but my argument is that they are more accurately studied in conjunction with the theme of mental,
emotional, and visual perspective. That is not to say that
these rich and idiosyncratic poetic images are neatly reduci-
ble to perspectivism. Rather, each is a separate inquiry into
the roots and consequences of fallen vision, and each expands
upon perspectivism in its own way, making its own connections between that motif and the more general Blakean
theme of the perceptual "family romance" of man, spectre,
and shadow.[11]

Perspective

Lawrence's description of the fall is strikingly close to
Blake's:

> When Adam went and took Eve, *after* the apple, he didn't
> do any more than he had done many a time before, in act.
> But in consciousness he did something very different. So did
> Eve. Each of them kept an eye on what they were doing, they
> watched what was happening to them. They wanted to
> KNOW. And that was the birth of sin. Not *doing* it, but
> KNOWING about it. Before the apple, they had shut their
> eyes and their minds had gone dark. Now, they peeped and
> pried and imagined. They watched themselves. And they felt
> uncomfortable after. They felt self-conscious. So they said,
> "The *act* is sin. Let's hide. We've sinned." [12]

After the sexual initiation of Tharmas and Enion in *The
Four Zoas,* Tharmas is enveloped by terror and is told by his
emanation:

> —Thy fear has made me tremble thy terrors have surrounded
>   me
> All Love is lost Terror succeeds & Hatred instead of Love
> And stern demands of Right & Duty instead of Liberty
> Once thou wast to Me the loveliest son of heaven—But now
> Why art thou Terrible and yet I love thee in thy terror till
> I am almost Extinct & soon shall be a Shadow in Oblivion
> Unless some way can be found that I may look upon thee &
>   live
> Hide me some Shadowy semblance. secret whispring in my
>   Ear
> In secret of soft wings. in mazes of delusive beauty
> I have lookd into the secret soul of him I lovd
> And in the Dark recesses found Sin & cannot return.
>   [I: 4: 17–27, E297] [13]

Weeping, Tharmas answers:

> Why wilt thou Examine every little fibre of my soul
> Spreading them out before the Sun like Stalks of flax to dry

> The infant joy is beautiful but its anatomy
> Horrible Ghast & Deadly nought shall thou find in it
> But Death Despair & Everlasting brooding Melancholy.
>
> [29–33]

Enion departs into nature, saying "Farewell I die I hide from thy searching eyes" (5:5).

As in Genesis, the initial fallen situation is of the lovers' looking upon each other for the first time and experiencing shame; but in Blake and Lawrence the sexual act precedes, rather than follows, the visual encounter. Seeing each other, Tharmas and Enion fall away from their embrace into a divided world, in which each becomes the other's object. Man's unifying faculty breaks down in dread as Tharmas discovers a sudden distance from his emanation and, simultaneously, a new feeling of himself as an object for her detached scrutiny. The new senses of detachment wither the beloved, as well as the self, examining, seizing the inmost form, reducing the human integrity into the atoms of its generative anatomy. This inquisitional eye is the accuser of sin, as it locates the horror of its own self-division in the portion that has split away. Such is the awakening of the perspectival eye, which weeps as soon as it opens, for what it sees is the remoteness of the beloved. The tears of Tharmas collect as the earthly ocean; the constant source of the material world is a reservoir of grief over the primal vanishing, and its waters are endlessly replenished by the banished emanation, who "weeps incessantly for my sin" (E467).

The perspectival eye, discovered in the fall of Tharmas, is the ruling principle of our experience, a fragmenting and rigidifying force that "condenses" human wholeness into "Nations & Peoples & Tongues" (J. III: 53: 8, E200). With its detached observation, its horizoned field, and its compartmentalization of experience into discrete pictures, it institutes our schismatic categories of space: above and below, here and there, before and behind, the outer of the bodily eye and the

inner of the mind's eye. In its search for a zenith viewpoint
that will include everything, it also moralizes space:

> But Urizen said Can I not leave this world of Cumbrous
>   wheels
> Circle oer Circle nor on high attain a void
> Where self sustaining I may view all things beneath my feet.
>   [F.Z. VI: 72: 22–24, E342]

So the paradise it conceives is a heaven which, as a topmost
level, must necessarily exist within the framework of lower,
non-paradisaical levels. In the perspectival orientation, holiness is a fragment and has but one place; and since the observer is not included in his own perspective, the place of
holiness must always be himself. Hence, jealousy and possessiveness are imbedded in his attitude toward the world:
"Such is self-love that envies all! a creeping skeleton / With
lamplike eyes watching around the frozen marriage bed"
(V.D.A.: 7: 21–22, E49). The hostility implicit in any viewpoint can reach in Blake a magnitude that makes Sartre's
freezing eye of *regard* seem almost benevolent by comparison: "They shrunk into their channels. dry the rocky strand
beneath his feet / Hiding themselves in rocky forms from the
Eyes of Urizen" (F.Z. VI: 68: 3–4, E338).

But the illusion of power and control conceals a radical
passivity. Under the dominion of the eye, we are never more
than witnesses. The natural world is a book of illustrations,
and the observer is like Rilke's king, in *The Notebooks of
Laurids Malte Brigge,* who found that "in turning the pages
one could never keep several pages in sight and that they
were fixed in their folios so that one could not shift them
about." [14] Seeing is limiting; Bachelard writes that "sight
curtails the dramas it witnesses. But a whiff of perfume, or
even the slightest odor can create an entire environment in the
world of the imagination." [15] Indeed, since our spectatorship
consists in the imposition of a predetermined, static field

upon the flux and diversity of the other, what we see is a
perpetual vanishing. Nature, whether Wordsworth's landscape of childhood or Los's Enitharmon, is intrinsically experienced as fading or moving away.[16] For one, like Urizen,
whose perspective is his empire, perception becomes a continual confrontation with the wreckage of what one has
built; the senses in this state are always giving way in favor
of memory:

> O what a world is here unlike those climes of bliss
> Where my sons gathered round my knees O thou poor ruind
>   world
> Thou horrible ruin once like me thou wast all glorious
> And now like me partaking desolate thy masters lot.
>   [F.Z.: VI: 72: 34–37, E342]

The senses also give way in favor of the sole self. Rousseau,
recognizing that perspectivism, both in drawing and seeing,
is not an instinctual but a sophisticated achievement, would
require his student, Emile, to draw perspectives in order to
learn about distance.[17] It would seem that the child's sense
of himself as separated from his environment must develop
to a certain strength before he is capable of seeing a horizoned field spread out before him. Eye and "I" develop
co-ordinately, and the existence of an object-world to be
naturalistically copied requires the existence of a perceiver
who is able to conceive of himself as a potential copyist. In
Rousseau this is a desirable passage in our education. In
Blake, however, the simultaneous development of eye and
self culminates in solipsism and paralysis, as the autonomous
eye comes to be aimed at the subject in the same detached
and hostile way in which it is directed at the other. Just as the
inquisitional eye of observation produces ever greater distance, taking the withered sense object into the void of mental abstraction, so the eye of self-observation withers man's
imaginative form, his creative activity, and finds its terminus

in stasis, emptiness, and despair. R. D. Laing describes self-consciousness as a sense of being under observation, a feeling which can generate the appearance of an independent being. Furthermore, "When the self partially abandons the body and its acts, and withdraws into mental activity, it experiences itself as an entity perhaps localized somewhere in the body." [18]—e.g., in the eye. In Blake the eye is the crippling double of the risen body, as self-consciousness is of the imagination. Tharmas and Enion, like Lawrence's Adam and Eve, fall into a world in which they are forever watching themselves. So they are left with the mere reflections of their full beings, a spectre and a shadow, in a state in which all acts and appearances are inevitably haunted by destructive counterparts.

Externalization

Blake's portrayal of the creation involves a crucial motif of externalization, and in *Jerusalem* the political theme of England's casting out of liberty is contextualized by a comprehensive imagery of separation, exile, and "scattering abroad." Externalization is usually figured as a separation from within the body: for example, Albion's Affections leave him through his loins, appearing "withoutside" (J. I: 19: 17, E162); and his sons are ripped loose from him in an agony of physical severance (15: 21–24, E158). So, also, the eyes, ears, nostrils, and tongue "roll outward," and "behold / What is within now seen without" (F.Z. II: 25: 22–24, E310). Behind Blake's motif stands Ezekiel's great theme of the Babylonian exile:

> I lifted up mine hand unto them also in the wilderness, that I would scatter them among the heathen, and disperse them through the countries. [20 : 23]

> As a shepherd seeketh out his flock in the day that he is among his sheep *that are* scattered; so will I seek out my sheep, and will deliver them out of all places where they have been scattered in the cloudy and dark day. [34 : 12]

In Blake, to turn outwards is to turn away not from the
inner but from a state of being in which a distinction between the two does not exist. Albion flees inward as his
children escape outward; the inner world of the individual
and the outer world of his natural and historical environment are twin births. And when Blake calls the unfallen
state "inner" or "within," he is not referring to mind or soul,
but means, instead, that all things were once embraced by
Albion's Edenic body. The process by which the embraced is
exiled into a separate space depends upon the Blakean theme
that the isolation of any force or faculty is itself an externalization, which polarizes man into, on the one hand, the accuser or the worshipper, and, on the other, the accused or the
worshipped. When the unfallen man fixes upon one element
in his imaginative life, becomes suddenly conscious of it
either in love or in fear, he objectifies that fragment of his
completeness, so cutting it off from the rest and giving it an
autonomous reality.

Such casting out is the work of the idol builder, and for
Blake the outer form is always a graven image. Wordsworth,
while thanking God for giving him idolatrous perception in
his childhood, describes the process of idolatry in a way that
Blake would have found accurate:

> Call ye these appearances—
> Which I beheld of shepherds in my youth,
> The sanctity of Nature given to man—
> A shadow, a delusion, ye who pore
> On the dead letter, miss the spirit of things;
> Whose truth is not a motion or a shape
> Instinct with vital functions, but a block
> Or waxen image which yourselves have made,
> And ye adore! But blessèd be the God
> Of Nature and of Man that this was so;
> That men before my inexperienced eyes
> Did first present themselves thus purified,
> Removed, and to a distance that was fit.
>
> [*The Prelude,* VIII: 293–305]

Blake might have given this passage whole to the Spectre of Urthona. We externalize the world of our experience by denying our responsibility in its creation. Furthermore, as fallen men, we are always aware of our fragmented status, and Blake says that our actions and desires inevitably express a desperation to recapture a lost completeness, to recapture, then, what we ourselves have cast out. But a man is reintegrated with his idol only on its own conditions: to consummate the Female Bliss offered by Enitharmon, Los realizes that he must enter Generation; and, in his annotations to Lavater, Blake approvingly marks many aphorisms on the general theme, "as the objects of his love, so the man." To worship a waxen image is to become like it; to make (or, synonymously in Blake, to perceive) the fallen body of the world is to assume one's own fallen body; we become what we behold.

"Behold" is the crucial word, for exiling involves a perceptual reorganization in which appearances are shifted into the dominion of the disengaged eye; as Urizen builds the Mundane Shell, he is comforted to see "The wondrous work flow forth like visible out of the invisible" (F.Z. II: 33: 10, E315). The land of exile is the space of visual perspective, and the spectre, or exiled form of the self, is a passive eye, an isolated subject interposed between the human and its emanation as a "reasoning negative." The process of objectification, however, does not stop with visibility, but continues into the night world of Ulro: so the webs in which Albion's Sons are trapped roll "outwards into darkness" (J. I: 7: 46, E149). Whatever is cut off from the self becomes increasingly estranged and unknown until it passes into the realm of the mysterious. In its final form, the spectre of man is a mental eye in abstract space living in a world of atoms and diagrams, combing the blanks between the stars for meaning, and feeling itself to be cast out in turn by an invisible Nobodaddy.

In his fall, Albion suffers three central experiences of exile. The first is the self-division caused by the casting out of Luvah and his emanation, Vala. The fall begins when the emotional energy of Luvah seizes the province of the reasoning mind and the visual where Urizen has fallen asleep. With Luvah's mission of conquest, which is in effect a self-exile, Albion's members lose their place within him. But Luvah's usurpation is really a journey of surrender in that an apparent intoxication with rational consciousness and the sense of sight has led him to abandon his proper sphere, that of man's desires and of the sense of smell, and to deliver up the thrust of Albion's emotional life to another psychic project than his own. Implicit in Luvah's act of idolatry is a sudden recognition that Urizen's province is external to his own and therefore subject to seizure, a sense of otherness born of the momentary cessation of Urizen's work, in the same way, for example, that any departure from normal functioning in the body will suddenly objectify the area of abnormality.

Since Albion's emotional force has abandoned the cooperation of his members and divided them against each other, the goal of that force, Vala's beauty, now appears outside, insofar as it has become an object of jealousy and competition. Urizen and Luvah struggle for something that is, for the first time, external to both of them; and in trying to straighten out a dispute within himself, Albion joins the strife on the side of the dispossessed Urizen and is thereby reduced to the form and status of the disputants. All man's being rushes into the mind, and "Entering into the Reasoning Power, forsaking Imagination / They become Spectres" (J. III: 74: 7–8, E227). The war ends as Luvah is cast out and given over to mortality as the subversive Orc, the dying and reviving god, whose sexual force serves an emanation now intrinsically alien, an enchantress, a visible and external nature. Man's desires have turned outward, the emotional foundations of an object-world have been established, and beauty has assumed a separate space.

Albion's second experience of externalization is an inevitable consequence of the first. His championing of Urizen is succeeded by his enthronement of the Zoa of the horizons as God, much as Shelley's Prometheus, the inventor of human reason, casts out his own rational consciousness by establishing Jupiter in the sky. In *Jerusalem* Blake is explicit that the Urizen whom Albion deifies as omnipotent Ruler is Satan, his own five-sense ratio in a detached and tyrannical form. So objectified, the spectre appears to Albion:

> Above him rose a Shadow from his wearied intellect:
> Of living gold, pure, perfect, holy: in white linen pure he
>   hoverd
> A sweet entrancing self-delusion a watry vision of Albion
> Soft exulting in existence; all the Man absorbing!
> Albion fell upon his face prostrate before the watry Shadow.
>   [II: 43: 37–41, E189]

Albion speaks "idolatrous to his own Shadow": "O I am nothing when I enter into judgment with thee! / If thou withdraw thy breath I die & vanish into Hades" (47–48). Through this act of self-abasement before a part of himself, Albion sets the precedent for all social conventions—religious, political, and moral—in which primacy is centralized in a figure, or figurehead, which is non-human and abstract but greater than a man.

When beauty and human responsibility have been cast out, so necessarily is Jerusalem, Albion's complete liberty. She is the form of human love, the emanation of Albion when he embraces all his faculties, as Vala is the form of natural love, the Courtly Mistress to whom man surrenders when he has turned away his own primacy. Since the creative freedom that Jerusalem embodies is the dangerous rival of the idolatry represented by Vala, she must be morally and intellectually disparaged as a deluding phantom and, more, as a sin; for she is, indeed, in the terms of the Decalogue, a false deity. Accordingly, the imagery of separation employed for her departure from Albion is one of a pushing away, a deliberate exiling, a hiding in shame. Blake's imagery clearly shows that all externalization is initiated by the subject as a putting of things from the self. In these lines, in his third shock of externalization, Albion violently purges himself of what he loves:

Hide thou Jerusalem in impalpable voidness, not to be
Touched by the hand nor seen with the eye: O Jerusalem
Would thou wert not & that thy place might never be found
Jerusalem! Jerusalem! deluding shadow of Albion!
Daughter of my phantasy! unlawful pleasure! Albions curse!
[J. I: 22: 26–28, 23: 1–2, E166]

Expansion and Contraction

As we observed in the story of the sacrifice, the percepts of the victim are withered, as well as distanced, when his senses are altered. Blake formulates this reaction as follows: "If Perceptive Organs vary: Objects of Perception seem to vary; / If the Perceptive Organs close: their Objects seem to close also" (J. II: 30: 55–56, E175). Similarly, Blake asks in *The Marriage:* "How do you know but ev'ry Bird that cuts the airy way, / Is an immense world of delight, clos'd by your senses five?" (7, E35). The closing of our perceptual possibilities to a visually dominated system of numerically limited natural organs closes the world of delight into the flying bird. Our bodily senses, Blake tells us, once possessed the power of contracting or expanding at will, but when Albion's perceptual organs solidified into two globed eyes, our objects were simultaneously englobed and, as in "The Mental Traveller," the flat earth became a ball. The Eternals, on the other hand, are not limited to a single mode of perception. Before the fall,

Earth was not: nor globes of attraction
The will of the Immortal expanded
Or contracted his all flexible senses.   [B.U.: 3: 36–38, E70]

When the eternal senses contract they behold "multitude,"
and when they expand they behold "As One Man all the
Universal family" (F.Z. I: 21: 2–4, E306). In a poem included in a letter to Butts, Blake proposes that the same
visionary mobility is an attainable potentiality of the bodily
eye:

My Eyes more & more
Like a Sea without shore
Continue Expanding
The Heavens commanding
Till the Jewels of Light
Heavenly Men beaming bright
Appeared as One Man.   [Oct. 2, 1800, E683]

Dependent upon such variation, the given form of the bird
is always provisional and does not limit how much we can see
of it. Blake never claims that the contracted perceptual mode
is without value, and he should never be misunderstood as
merely an enemy of all abstraction, much less of all perspective. He is, rather, the enemy of any project in which reality
is solely, or most authoritatively, delineated by those modes.
In Eternity, the reorganized senses retain every capacity they
now have, but no one capacity is final, and there is a complete
register of possibilities at the spontaneous service of desire.
Indeed, a perceptual fluidity is necessary for the direct appre-
ciation of both the uniqueness of minute identities and their
unified organization as the body of one man. In fallen perception, we can see multitude and think unity, but, when
there is such a split between seeing and thinking, multitude
becomes fragmentation and unity becomes vague generaliza-
tion.

Blake uses two figures—which are two states organized by

the mercy of Los—for the loss of our original vision. One
is the State of Adam, or man's physical stature, a Limit of
Contraction beyond which form cannot shrink. Even though
the mind can further reduce the bird to a hypothetical
particle, a grain of sand among other identical grains, the
visible form of the bird is established as a point of ultimate
contraction for the senses. The other is the State of Satan, or
rock, a Limit of Opacity beyond which the barriers to our
perception cannot be intensified. Mentally and emotionally,
we can become absorbed in opacity, seeing nothing but the
same increasingly meaningless grain of sand and, more, living
in what Rilke called a "night without objects"; [19] but such
total obscurity does not characterize the phenomenal world,
where we have not yet lost the surfaces, although in immediate perception they block each other off and conceal from
us even the full visibility of the object. The process of contraction is particularly well exhibited as Los, hammering out
the hardened, static forms of the natural eye, becomes as
his creations are: his movements suddenly assume a spas-
modic quality, and he reacts to his new muscular fibers with
a writhing dance, "stamping the Abyss" (F.Z. II: 556: 24–31,
E331). The fall into mortality is a rigidification, finally completed in the immobility of the corpse, the form in which
the Limits of Adam and Satan converge.

Perceptual fluidity is lost when the object of perception is
given primacy, the perceiver losing flexibility through quite
literally being tied to the object. In directing his eyes toward
what is in front of him, fixing them upon the external object
as if he were hypnotized by it, he closes himself into what
Blake calls the single vision of "Newton's sleep." But contraction is simultaneously an emotional problem, for our
perceptive organs close specifically upon objects that seem to
embody our desires. We are lured into nature, pursuing
Vala, the "lovely form / That drew the body of Man from
heaven into this dark Abyss" (F.Z. V: 59: 1–2, E333). But

the closed object can only be a source of frustration, for Blake reiterates that human love cannot be restricted to a visible globe or a mental point or even the spectral being of another person; these are not forms adequate either to the desire and imagination of the subject or the completeness of the beloved. In a Notebook lyric, Blake speaks at once of emotional relationship, perception, and social convention:

> Why should I be bound to thee
> O my lovely mirtle tree
> Love free love cannot be bound
> To any tree that grows on ground.   [E460]

However, the responsibility for his frustration rests with the perceiver, for we bind ourselves, and Blake shows that our relations with a separate object-world are characterized by a grasping possessiveness, a tying of objects to the self. It is not mere selfishness that Blake is speaking of, and something much more comprehensive than the possessiveness of the miser. It may be noted that the love borne to the idol Vala is specifically a desire to possess her and that, as a whole, the dismemberment of Albion proceeds by a series of attempts to annex what has been externalized. In Blake the fallen ego in every man, denying any connection outside itself, is forced to relate to the objects of its desire in an acquisitive mode, and the same possessiveness characterizes fallen perception. Here too we must belong and / or have belongings; as Rilke writes, "Anxiously we clamor for a hold." [20] The fragments must be bound together, and so we bind tightly to ourselves what is felt to be remote from us over an inevitable stretch of pure distance, what is constantly in danger of vanishing in the horizoned organization of the "real" and the "present." We can only relate to our objects by accumulating them; thus the sun we see is "somewhat like a guinea." Erdman's treatment of the spectral social modes of capitalism, property, and colonialism in *Blake: Prophet Against Empire* enriches our understanding of the Blakean selfhood as an empire in microcosm.

For fallen man, all acts of relationship are fundamentally imperialistic, and the expansion of consciousness itself becomes Faustian, a quest for the secret or key, and an invasion of the hidden depths of the other with the purpose of taking control. But, as in "The Crystal Cabinet" (E479), the possessor is ultimately accumulated by his idol. In this lyric, the speaker, overwhelmed by the shining clarity of the new moony night, attempts to seize the "inmost Form" of the translucent maiden and so finds himself in the landscape of Ulro as a weeping babe in the wilds, with his maiden now a "Weeping Woman." In *Jerusalem,* the myrtle tree is finally revealed as the Tree of Mystery, the obscure and forbidden Source, worshipped as the locus of all the forces external to consciousness that seem to compel spectral man.

The human image of our normative perceptual contraction is the sleep of Albion, who has forsaken Jerusalem and bound himself to Vala. His sleep is the repose desired by Urizen, the freedom from the necessity to organize and create. Yet it is the most fitful and tortured of reposes, because things continue to happen; but while everything once happened within the participation of the Eternal Humanity, now everything happens beyond his sleeping faculties: things merely pass over him in dreams; things now happen *to* him. He has become pure object to the forces of nature, a rock among other rocks. The hypnosis of Vala rigidly contracts the eyes to a single direction and is fully achieved when the eyes close and the subject falls asleep.

The Vortex

In the vortex Blake synthesizes the figures of externalization and contraction and gives us his fullest account of the

mechanics of perspectival observation. The vortex is most
elaborately described in the episode of Milton's descent to
the World of Death:

> The nature of infinity is this: That every thing has its
> Own Vortex; and when once a traveller thro' Eternity
> Has passd that Vortex, he percieves it roll backward behind
> His path, into a globe itself infolding; like a sun:
> Or like a moon, or like a universe of starry majesty,
> While he keeps onwards in his wondrous journey on the
> earth
> Or like a human form, a friend with whom he livd benevo-
> lent.
> As the eye of man views both the east & west encompassing
> Its vortex; and the north & south, with all their starry host;
> Also the rising sun & setting moon he views surrounding
> His corn-fields and his valleys of five hundred acres square.
> Thus is the earth one infinite plane, and not as apparent
> To the weak traveller confin'd beneath the moony shade.
> Thus is the heaven a vortex passd already, and the earth
> A vortex not yet pass'd by the traveller thro' Eternity.
>
> First Milton saw Albion upon the Rock of Ages,
> Deadly pale outstretchd and snowy cold, storm coverd;
> A Giant form of perfect beauty outstretchd on the rock
> In solemn death: the Sea of Time & Space thunderd aloud
> Against the rock, which was inwrapped with the weeds of
> death
> Hovering over the cold bosom, in its vortex Milton bent
> down
> To the bosom of death, what was underneath soon seemd
> above.
> A cloudy heaven mingled with stormy seas in loudest ruin;
> But as a wintry globe descends precipitant thro' Beulah
> bursting,
> With thunders loud, and terrible: so Miltons shadow fell,
> Precipitant loud thundring into the Sea of Time & Space.

Then first I saw him in the Zenith as a falling star,
Descending perpendicular, swift as the swallow or swift.

[M. I: 15: 21–48, E108]

The vortex is discussed at length and with accompanying
diagram by Adams, who treats it as an image of imaginative
experience cast in terms of the eyes, since the eyes are "mundane symbols for types of imaginative powers." [21] In a
way, Adams falls into Blake's trap. Using visual analogues
and spatial diagrams for imagination leads him to describe
the rays of the vortex as infinitely extending into a "world
of mind." Although this intimates that the imagination expands according to visual laws, a diagram is not wholly in-
appropriate here, since Blake is actually describing not
imaginative but visual experience. Still, no diagram can
include the motion of the vortex—the inexorable spiral
that most immediately characterizes it as a phenomenon—nor
account for the boldness of Blake's metaphor. By likening
visual perception to a plunge through a whirlpool, Blake
intimates that the very process of observation is a situation
of extreme anxiety.

We can advance our understanding of this complicated
figure if we consider it in the context of Blake's general
imagery of fallen perception. Blake represents the relationship of perceiver and perceived as a perspectival cone, which
is not static, as a diagram would imply it to be, but which
draws us through the object so that it rolls back behind us
in the shape of a distant globe. The globes are the distant
stars of the Zodiac seen in the night sky, as well as the "atoms
of Democritus" (E469) and the homogeneous particles of
grain ground through Satan's Mill of reductive reasoning;
so, also, the summary image of the space of our own dwelling
is a globed earth beneath a domed sky. In the vortex, we
progress through a spiraling circularity into the perception
of circular objects; and the circularity of both perceptual

process and percept is determined by the fact that the organs
of perspectival experience, the natural eyes, are themselves
globular, as is our field of perception, which is horizoned
along a circular periphery. The earth is round because our
field of perception is round. Both object and organ have
been contracted and englobed: we become what we behold,
we are as we perceive, we perceive what we are, "He who sees
the Ratio only sees himself only."

When Milton has passed the vortex of heaven, when
therefore he no longer lives among the things of heaven but
sees them behind and above in distant stars and planets, he
receives his first view of the earth—in fact, his first *view* of
anything. What he sees is the Eternal Humanity from the
zenith perspective in which it will always appear as a narrow
rock in the sea. But where our eyes are focused, we too,
through the whirlpool, come to be situated with a new
vortex before us; so to see Albion as an island is to enter a
second whirlpool through which one plunges into the Sea of
Time and Space, where even the zenith perspective, as a
bodily possibility, is lost. And as the metaphor is fully un-
raveled in a magnificent perspectival reversal, Milton sees an
ocean from the zenith and, having fallen, looks back to the
zenith, which is itself now ocean-like. Thus, what was before
rolls behind, "what was underneath soon seemd above."
What is before the eyes, as a sea of sheer matter, necessarily
comes behind them in an indistinct welter of mental abstractions, or Urizen's cloudy heaven. Further, at the same
time as Milton falls from the zenith, he becomes visible
from the earth, appearing as a falling star; to regard objec-
tively is to become objectified. Milton enters the World of
Death and becomes one of us, then, by assuming a visible and
visually oriented organization. Taking up a vantage point, he
enters the globular field of our perception in the shape of a
"wintry globe."

In this passage, the vortex, although it purports to describe "the nature of infinity," actually portrays the collapse of infinity into limits and fragments. Milton has chosen to enter the fallen world, and he can do so only by giving himself to a descent in consciousness. In his other major passage on the vortex, Blake is more explicit that the vortex is a structure of Error, not of complete vision. Here, in *The Four Zoas,* Urizen journeys through his dens, setting up perspectives to order the abyss: "Creating many a Vortex fixing many a Science in the deep" (VI: 72: 13, E342). When Urizen comes to where a vortex ceases to operate, everything appears to him upward, both behind and before him. He has descended, but before him is an uphill space of void. Setting up a vortex, he makes this space downward; his difficult journey thus can progress with ease, and he can continue to fall. An unbearable chaos is given a structure through reactive creativity, and Urizen can advance in his downward search for a perfect zenith, which, when he finds it, becomes not a resting place but another terrifying abyss that has to be perspectivally structured. So Urizen creates a world of globes and spreads his mantle "from Vortex to Vortex." Here, again, the motion of the vortex is important, for the vortices in this image are wheels—"the turning wheels of heaven"—suggesting the mechanical heaven of deism, the clock wheels set in motion by the Clockmaker God. The circling of the whirlpool becomes a cycle, a zodiacal revolution, a Spindle of Destruction. And in *Jerusalem* the vortex is a trap into which Hyle (the man of material nature) draws the sons of Jerusalem inwards toward Babylon.

In unfallen perception the vortex exists in potential, rather than operation. The perceiver "encompasses" the vortex, rather than being encompassed by it, as Milton and Urizen are. Subject and object appear on the same infinite flat plane, and Blake maintains that in this way the earth appears flat, rather than globular, in redeemed vision. But a vortex may open under the perceiver's feet, as it were; and objects will now appear no longer on his plane, but on a different one below him. What was a single surface then becomes the uppermost ring of the whirlpool waters. Threefold nature appears in the three-dimensional depth perception of the perspectival field. The perceiver is suddenly on a different level of being from his objects, and his necessary fall into the emptiness beneath him is the fall into nature. To enter an object's vortex, then, is to perceive the object at a distance with a detached mind at one end, an independent point of visibility at the other, and a stretch of pure space, or void, between as an inherent part of the structure. When perception is so organized, percepts take on a wholly discrete character, unrelated to the viewer or to each other, and what was once close and friendly moves away from us as a collection of random globes in empty space. Furthermore, every viewpoint is lost as soon as it is taken; even though he may choose it, the observer immediately loses control of his cognitive position. To assume a viewpoint is necessarily to slide through the cone into a radically altered field of objects. One vortex inevitably leads to another, and each vortical journey represents a further distancing of the globes, until they attain the invisible, mental reality of Democritus' atoms.

The vortex, as a whirlpool of material waters and as a devouring mouth, like those of the Covering Cherub and Rahab, produces the material bodies in which actuality is felt in the fallen world to subsist; and among these products is the human body, for when the vortex of any object is entered, the perceiver himself assumes the configuration of a visible, material object, and his own body becomes one of the globes that is estranged from him. Thus, through the vortex, he spirals into his cavern. Gleckner is quite accurate, then, in simultaneously treating the image of the cavern and that of the vortex, but his diagrammatic equation of the two is misleading because it does not make clear that there is no cavern until the apex of visibility is passed. However, he does intimate valuably that perceptual organs, the cavern chinks, are themselves objects to the Urizenic mind's eye. And since both eye and object are whirlpools to swallow each other, it would seem, as Adams and Frye observe, that a passage through the vortex results in shaping existence as an hourglass with two halves—the inner and outer, soul and body, spirit and matter, and so forth—and a nexus between, brain to Frye and (better) cavern chink to Adams.[22] But what all three formulations seem to miss is that, as a whole, the presentation of the vortex contains a certain irony. The figure is in all probability a parody of the Cartesian theory of vortices,[23] and although Urizen interprets the vortex as the absolute structure of vision, and Blake in *Milton* tempts the reader to do the same, we cannot forget that Blake uses the image only to describe the process of falling. For Blake, a world characterized by *a priori* and diagrammatic patterns of experience is necessarily a fallen one. To take up the vortex that is potential in any act of perception is to restrict one's vision to perspective; to see in this way is to live in a world of cycles, hourglasses, spindles, and whirlpools, and it is also to fall continuously through empty space.

The visible globe can serve as a nexus, however, not between the two segments of the hourglass—fallen nature and fallen mind—but between the hourglass as a whole and the infinity that existed before the vortex began to operate. Every vortical percept is a minute particular, which can be opened up again by altering the organization of faculties which in the first place englobed it. Milton's work, once he has entered the Vortex of the Dead and there become incarnated, is to take up the globes and expand them by severing the sense of their reality from the limits of their visibility. Thus, throughout his labors, Los holds in his hands a fiery Globe of Blood: what the eye and mental eye take as a discrete particle of man's matter will appear, in its expanded form, as the new human body in its wholeness, bursting through the constraints of the mundane appearances. So, at the Last Judgment, a fiery sun of wrath leaves its natural course to consume sky and earth. The distant globes suddenly approach with an energy and a direction that contradict the dynamics of the vortex and so destroy it.

Center and Circumference

One of Blake's most demanding structures, the image of the center and circumference, like the vortex, is crucially ironic. To try to find a way out in the given terms of the figure is to slip into a trap, for the differentiation between center and circumference is itself the target of Blake's attack. It is only when the unity of the Zoas collapses that the image comes into being: "All fell towards the Center, sinking downwards in dire ruin" (J. III: 59: 17, E206); and the newly created center is our fallen world, "the sublime Universe of Los & Enitharmon."

In Blake the form of an act conditions the form of its consequences. Since Luvah's seizure of the horses of light is an assertion of himself as a center for all existence, man in his fallen selfhood becomes a center: his perception is now egocentric, because his habitual point of relation is his own perspective, which he universalizes. And that acts of perception are simultaneously expressions of emotion is made clear in a description of the Satanic heart in *Jerusalem* as a "white Dot calld a Center from which branches out / A Circle in continual gyrations" (29: 17–24, E173). In the passage, the one who contemplates this "Devouring Power" becomes its food: the subject is swallowed by the vortex of the natural object; or his viewpoint can itself be a mouth to devour his objects and grind them into homogeneous particles.

We are centers, and we see centers. The sublime universe is a collection of viewpoints which deny each other and which, further, find their ultimate forms as abstract points in pure space. The earth itself is reduced to a point, in that as a full globe it exists in the mind, rather than in the senses. Blake often pictures the center as the Ark of the Holy of Holies, for it is man's centrality, the secret "white dot" of his self-hood, that is the creative source of his fallen world. Indeed, natural existence is a centralized one in all its particulars: the Philosophy of Five Senses is a centralization of cognitive possibility; perspectivism is a visual centralization; Urizen is a centralization of holiness; a tyrant is a centralization of power; a natural heart fixed in its affection to a naturalized emanation is a centralization of emotion. Man, in his spectral body of self-love and self-consciousness, is a totally closed center: "Beyond the bounds of their own self their senses cannot penetrate" (F.Z. VI: 70a: 12, E340).

The Sanctuary of Eden, Blake tells us, is in the circum-ference, and the outline is the signal of the wholeness and the unique identity of an achieved desire. But the fixed and isolated center—the mental and emotional viewpoint of the self and the field it generates—is described in the following image as an emptiness, one's non-identity and non-achieve-ment. Here, in Blake's parallel to the infernal assembly of *Paradise Lost,* Book II, centralization is presented as a mode of power, with which the fallen Eternals respond to the shattering of their world:

> From every-one of the Four Regions of Human Majesty,
> There is an Outside spread Without, & an Outside spread Within
> Beyond the Outline of Identity both ways, which meet in One:
> An orbed Void of doubt, despair, hunger, & thirst & sorrow.
> Here the Twelve Sons of Albion, join'd in dark Assembly,
> . . . . .
> To murder their own Souls, to build a Kingdom among the Dead.   [J. I: 18: 1–10, E161]

A center point may appear to be a solid and stationary base, but in Blake's world of energy, in which the individuated is always driven toward some kind of completion, it is highly unstable, for there are no true bases, only types of movement. Any motion from a center, any quest for relationship that takes the self as its point of orientation, can only lead into the final solipsism of Ulro. This Urizen discovers when he journeys through his dens in Night VI, desperately trying to expand his center to the limits of the universe and achieving only increasingly fearful confirmations of nonentity.

The Assembly passage contains in its second and third lines an image that may appear particularly forbidding. The center is the meeting point of two outsides, that of the fallen mind and that of the fallen body. As noted in the discussion of externalization, by "outside" Blake means outside Albion. We are also told that the center is beyond the Outline of Identity both ways—or the identity of inner and outer in Albion's unfallen form. Elsewhere Blake elaborates upon this radically non-spatial figure:

> What is Above is Within, for every-thing in Eternity is trans-
>   lucent:
> The Circumference is Within: Without, is formed the Selfish
>   Center
> And the Circumference still expands going forward to Eter-
>   nity.   [J. III: 71: 6–8, E222]

In the "Ancient Poets" passage of *The Marriage,* Blake places all gods and paradises, which we instinctively locate beyond the horizons, inside the human breast, and in the same way he finds the Outline of Identity inside the center. The "Within" Blake speaks of is then directly opposed to the "Outside spread Within" in which Urizen travels; it is the imagination as opposed to the mind. As a center, man can regard outwards from his own centrality, in which case he arrives at the larger enclosing center of the Mundane Shell;

he can reflect inwards, by introspection, upon his own centrality, in which case he enters his own abyss; or he can
look within his own center to his imagination, where he can
find a new world, the same as the one beyond the Mundane
Shell:

> The Vegetative Universe, opens like a flower from the Earths
>   center:
> In which is Eternity. It expands in Stars to the Mundane
>   Shell
> And there it meets Eternity again, both within and without.
>   [J. I: 13: 34–36, E155]

Here the fallen world is an expanse interposed between two
eternities. It is a barrier, the positive space between eye and
object, the distance between desire and fulfillment, the separation of sensation and synthesis. The source of any object—for
example, a flower—is the eternity within the earth's center,
for all beginnings are in Eden: "This World is too poor to
produce one Seed" (Ann. to Reynolds, E646). Similarly, this
world is too poor to accommodate the full growth and the
achieved being of the object. The things of imagination are
not available to our five senses or their ratio, and Blake
figures their totality as a world in a grain of sand, Heaven in
a wild flower:

> Thou percievest the Flowers put forth their precious Odours!
> And none can tell how from so small a center comes such
>   sweets
> Forgetting that within the Center Eternity expands
> Its ever during doors.   [M. II: 31: 46–49, E130]

The center is the East of Luvah and is "unapproachable
for ever" (J. I: 12: 56, E154). As the Ark of the Holy of
Holies, it is unapproachable in that the expansive energy
embodied in Luvah is forbidden under the Urizenic dispensation. But it is in another way unapproachable, for the
Urizenic eye regards the possibility of a world within a point

as a phantom of an overheated brain. Within the center, the
abstract dot in diagrammatic space, are all the human faculties exiled from a domain of perspectivism, empiricism, and
rationalism. It is the dimension of the devalued and of the
repressed, and it should be noted that in Blake not only
men but external objects, such as flowers, have such a dimension. Thus, Beulah, the state of pleasures and dreams, is
located "Beneath the bottoms of the Graves, which is Earths
central joint" (J. II: 48: 13, E194). So too it is the job of Los
to open the unapproachable center of the natural object:

> And every Generated Body in its inward form,
> Is a garden of delight & a building of magnificence,
> Built by the Sons of Los.   [M. I: 26: 31–33, E122]

His city Golgonooza is located in the center, built on the
omphalos of London Stone; and here Los creates his children,
or works of art: "Every one a translucent Wonder: a Universe within" (J. I: 14: 17, E157).

In Eden, center and circumference are fused as fire and its
outline, one non-existent without the other. But Albion's
outline, after he has fallen from it, is solidified into a Devourer, a pre-existent global field, while the true circumference is suppressed within the translucent world of the
center. Since the outward circumference represents actual
contour, to shape creations in terms of it (Blake might give
Augustan couplet versification as an example of this) is to
feed the Devourer and sacrifice to Vala one's potentially
renovative energy. Los's work is, rather, to expand the world
within the point, to cultivate it until it becomes for us a
counter-world, equal in credibility to that of the diagram.
Any object and any organ is such a point in a world where
the perceiver himself is a center point. As in the vortex, in
which the way back is through the image but not in terms
of it, so in the case of the center and the circumference: every
globe that rolls backwards from the apex of visibility is a

nexus, not *in* itself, but *within* itself. While once the universal imagination contained all, now it is, itself, contained within each of its fragments. It is one of the most striking features of Blake's mythology that every fallen entity, animal and inanimate as well as human, has what corresponds structurally to an unconscious, within which its unfallen completeness, or humanity, still survives and is potentially available to our senses.

Blake's climactic image of the imprisoned outline is that of Jerusalem in the stomach of the Covering Cherub, the total form of liberty within the total form of prohibition. And when at last Albion arises and walks into heaven, he leaves the globed womb where he has slept, or breaks out of the center in a new birth. Then the Covering Cherub, as the space between two eternities, vanishes, literally cancelled by the resurrection, and the center and the circumference return to each other as flame to its form.

Hermaphrodite

The structures of perception described in the previous sections develop an image of a body organized according to the perspectival mind's eye, which, regarding from self, can see only forms independent of itself and potentially hostile to its desires for universalization. Everything in Blake's poetic world seeks expansion; each fragment seeks a personal absoluteness through intellectual imposition or material appropriation and so absorbs other forms into itself. Claiming universality, it cannot abide the similar programs of other fragments. There is only mutual negation, or devouring, and the state of dissension implicit in the subject-object schism of Generation realizes itself in the ultimate nightmares of Ulro, where each succeeds in finding his own world. The final manifestation of the devouring body of conflict, the Covering Cherub with Jerusalem in its stomach, is Blake's Antichrist, the dragon that bars us from paradise with its

fiery sword, and a summary form of all that is opposed to
Albion's Edenic life. But why is it so difficult for the caverned
man to break with the mechanisms that produce the Cherub?

The Cherub makes its most extensive appearance in the
final chapter of *Jerusalem,* where it is described as a compos-
ite of body and church, of natural landscape and ravaging
empire, a "majestic image / Of Selfhood," devouring "the
rejected corse of death": "His Head dark, deadly, in its Brain
incloses a reflexion / Of Eden all perverted" (see 89: E245–
47). Egypt, Rome, and Babylon are such reflections, purely
mental and deranged versions of paradise; and in every detail the Cherub is a perverted reflection of the new body of
Albion that Blake describes in the poem's closing plates.
Blind, opaque, absorbing everything into itself, it is a "Body
put off," a deadly parody of the increase of perception, in
which the senses are finally closed.

But perhaps most critically, its "terrible indefinite Hermaphroditic form" parodies the androgynous being of the
risen Albion. The Cherub is a completed form: its loins
enclose Babylon, and Jerusalem is hidden in its stomach.
Blake frequently describes fallen institutions and patterns of
behavior as hermaphroditic amalgams in which one sex is
hidden within or absorbed by the other. So in *The Four Zoas*
the war around Jerusalem's gate is perceived as a "Vast
Hermaphroditic form" laboring with convulsive groans to
give birth to Satan, "a male without a female counterpart,"
the embodiment of utterly unfulfillable desire and, thus, of
eternal despair (see VIII: 104a: 19–28, E363). So, also, Rahab
is the Accuser's "Feminine Power unreveal'd" and sits deep
within the monstrous body of Druidism (J. III: 70: 18, E222).
A female in a male, a male in a female—religion hidden in
war, liberty imprisoned, Albion in the nets of Vala—these are
Blake's ultimate figures of the incorporation of man into the
given, a marriage of spectre and shadow, Satan and Rahab,
that stands between the true spousal partners, Albion and

Jerusalem, and thus keeps us from paradise, like a dragon with a flaming sword.

If in all our acts we create our bodies, then the Cherub stands as the ideal image to which fallen man commits his self-transformations. Shelley's hermophrodite in *The Witch of Atlas* can help us understand why Blake's monster holds such power. Built from fire and snow, the "sexless" Hermaphrodite represents the limits of both success and failure in the Witch's magic. A figure in which all opposites are reconciled, it is also perfected in its inwardness: its eyes are "unawakened"; "And o'er its gentle countenance did play / The busy dreams, as thick as summer flies" (362–64). But its dominant feature is perhaps its lack of human energy, and, for all its magnificence, it is finally not sufficient to the sustained interest of either the Witch or the poet, as it is simply left behind by the poem's narrative.

Like Shelley's beautiful and sterile artifice, and like, too, the new man manufactured by Victor Frankenstein, Blake's Cherub expresses not the diabolical force in a Manichean dualism, but, in a distorted way, the Romantic desire to create improved life. For the Romantics, the condition of all fallen action is the drive to reach Eden, and in Blake this is a longing so fierce that his characters are depicted as utterly singleminded in their quest to produce new worlds and new bodies, every one an image of paradise. The Hermaphrodite represents this desire gone astray, and it belongs to the tradition of the beautiful hell, or Bower of Bliss: the grot of Keats's Belle Dame, the Crystal Cabinet, the solitude of Shelley's Alastor. These parodies of Eden are perverted reflections not only of pleasure, but also of the deep condition of pleasure, that of reunification. In them, subject and object, fire and ice, or male and female seem to come together, but in such a way that the distinctions between the two are obliterated. Blake's non-sexual Hermaphrodite provides a version of reunification that is the antithesis of poetic creation, a reconciliation in which the energetic interplay of contraries is ended and, indeed, one contrary simply swallows the other.

Frye remarks that the spectral parodies, or Divine Analogies, of imagination depend for their appeal upon a confusion of similitude and identity.[24] The Cherub resembles the risen body; hallucination resembles poetic enthusiasm; violence resembles love. These are similarities that Blake's fallen man is only too anxious to accept, for they are not only reflections of the Edenic, but desperate expressions of his need for it. For this reason the parodies are often portrayed so convincingly that they may at moments persuade the reader. Vala's love, for example, is an entrapment and Jerusalem's, a liberation, but they are irresistibly like each other. Thus, Enitharmon's song of Female Love in *The Four Zoas* juxtaposes snatches of Oothoon's chant of emancipation—

> Arise you little glancing wings & sing your infant joy
> Arise & drink your bliss
> For everything that lives is holy   [II: 34: 78–80, E317]

—to blatantly antithetical sentiments:

> The joy of woman is the Death of her most best beloved
> Who dies for Love of her
> In torments of fierce jealousy & pangs of adoration.   [63–65]

Blake expresses the workings of Analogy most succinctly in *Jerusalem* when he calls natural love "a pretence of love to destroy love" (I: 17: 26, E160). False similitude is then one kind of blockage in the doors of perception. Los, in *Jerusalem,* is the exposer of parodies; his art removes the superficial resemblance of the Satanic to the Edenic and thereby deprives the former of its hypnotic hold over us.

We can take the notion of Divine Analogy a step further by examining the ways in which parodies are created. The problem touches on the nature of metaphor in Blake's poetry and the role of literalism in the reader's response to it. In some ways, Blake demands that we take metaphors literally, that we believe, for instance, that counterrevolutionary England is a repetition of Babylon or that we can achieve a resurrected body that is not merely a spiritualization of the given. On the other hand, Blake is equally insistent that the identification of phenomena that simply resemble each other is an abstraction that leads to an inferno of indistinguishable grains of sand. In any instance of relationship in Blake we must separate a correct from a misplaced literalism. England is literally the diminished body of Albion, and Albion, also literally, is called upon to expand. To expand in natural terms, to enlarge his dimensions over the earth, would be imperialism, which is the parody of the kind of expansion Blake intends. Albion must expand from the given, not in terms of it; the metaphor calls us into a new dimension of being. To actualize the metaphor in the conditions of our own time and space is to translate the imaginative into the natural, not to raise ourselves to Eden but to bring it down to our level. In this way the desire for a resurrection gives birth to the Hermaphrodite.

Such projects of actualization are often described in terms of will or mere force: of "corporeal command" that leads us to literalize the notion of sacrifice as murder, as the Druids do; of instituting Eden by personal fiat, as Urizen does; of manufacturing paradise, as Newton does, with technological water-wheels that parody the wheels-within-wheels of Ezekiel's Divine Chariot. Blake's Eden cannot be forced or programmed, even by Los; for spontaneity is as vital to Blake as it is to the later Romantics. In the form of prophetic commitment, the will can serve the purposes of poetic creation, but acting by itself, as it does in the natural world of "Female Will," it can produce only Ulro. This is equally true of the creative capacities of reason and emotion, when they function in isolation. Indeed, the parody can be described as a paradise created by any component of fallen man other than the imagination.

It can also be described as the appearance of paradise from any fallen point of view. Such a partial comprehension distorts the Edenic into its negation; and, in so doing, it satirizes the viewpoint itself. Blake's fallen man is an unwitting parodist, trapped in the multiplying ironies of his own creations. Luvah is twisted into Satan, as emotional vitality survives in Mosaic and Pauline moralism in the vehemence brought to the denunciation of sin. Tharmas, the power of the body to fulfill all impulses, is twisted into the Cherub, which both paralyzes us and is in itself a configuration of utter powerlessness. The cave parodies the openness of Jerusalem, and gradually the prisoner transforms himself into the dead matter that encloses him.

It is finally difficult to gauge Blake's elusive and endlessly suggestive satire: how much, for instance, in Enitharmon's parody of Oothoon is fraudulent masquerade and how much, tragic self-deception. In either case, Blake is unsparing in his insistence that we see through the parody to the love that it destroys. The hermaphroditic Cherub incarnates our enslavement, and its structural resemblances to the risen body suggest that, to a great extent, what keeps us from Eden is our vulnerability to its simulations. It appears to us that the Cherub's flaming sword stands in our way, but the final irony, to which all Blake's structures of perception point, is that there is nothing in the character of existence that actually compels us to remain outside paradise.

CHAPTER 3

Renovation

The Artist

It might seem that Blake's critique of the natural world is so complete that any story of its redemption must introduce, through some form of transcendence, factors outside that world. This is, indeed, a temptation to which Blake's characters often fall prey. But the crux in his myth is that redemptive potentiality exists within nature, specifically in the fallen artist and in the fallen senses.

The interdependence of the two is clearly established in *The Marriage,* where Blake claims that the apocalypse of sensual enjoyment requires the elimination of the dualism of body and soul: "this I shall do by printing in the infernal method, by corrosives, which in Hell are salutary and medicinal, melting apparent surfaces away and displaying the infinite which was hid" (14, E38). Blake thought of his "infernal" method of engraving, in which the acid bites away not the lines of the burin but the areas between them, as analogous to the demiurgic furnaces of Los, in which all our percepts are hammered into form.[1] Los's furnaces are probably modeled on that of Ezekiel, in which the Lord's fury melts away the dross of the House of Israel (22:18–22); and there Blake shows us cannons, works of art, our five senses, and a reawakened Albion all emerging from the same source, all products of the same human faculty in different phases of self-recognition. Blake is to be taken literally when he writes: "The Nature of my Work is Visionary or Imaginative it is an Endeavour to Restore [what the Ancients called] the Golden Age" (V.L.J., E545). And the goal of Los's labor is the resurrection of the body, as it was also the goal of Ezekiel, who raised dry bones with his inspired words.

Accusation and Forgiveness

The process of redemption is most completely detailed in *Jerusalem,* as the fall is most fully presented in *The Four Zoas.* In the final epic, renovation takes the form of a conflict of two forces, accusation and forgiveness. I would suggest that the orthodoxy usually implicit in these concepts can lead readers away from the nature of the poem, for the terms have to do essentially with the body and with art. Blake is not concerned with vices, but with deadly failures in vision, and accusation and forgiveness are treated not, exactly, as moral ideas, nor even as emotions, but as postures of the imagination toward the objects of perception.

Accusation comprehends all structures of negation, which push things away from us, purging them as sins and distancing them as far as possible from the pure, holy palace of the self. The philosophical form of accusation is skepticism, the doubt with which any empiricism regards information attributable neither to the five senses nor to reasoning upon them. Less explicitly, it also includes any idealism, rationalism, or transcendentalism which disparages the organs of sense and, indeed, any epistemological project that organizes human possibilities in a hierarchical class-structure:

> The Spectre is the Reasoning Power in Man; & when separated
> From Imagination, and closing itself as in steel, in a Ratio
> Of the Things of Memory. It thence frames Laws & Moralities
> To destroy Imagination! the Divine Body, by Martyrdoms &
>   Wars.   [J. III: 74: 10–13, E227]

In its moral masquerade, spectral reason becomes Satan, the divine Accuser of Transgression, who brands as evil all desires for a human expansion that would lift man out of the fallen world. In his annotations to Lavater, Blake defines an act as any fulfillment of desire that does not hinder similar fulfillment in another or serve in effect as a prohibition or diminishment to oneself (E590). Any true act subverts the imprisoning reign of the spectre, as any refusal to act reinforces it. So the work of the visionary poet, based outside the five-sense system, is accused:

> Every Emanative joy forbidden as a Crime:
> And the Emanations buried alive in the earth with pomp of
>   religion:
> Inspiration deny'd; Genius forbidden by laws of punishment!
>   [J. I: 9: 14–16, E150]

The act most available to natural man is sexuality, and this, since it breaks down the worshipper-idol relationship, is vehemently accused: "They suppose that Womans Love is Sin. in consequence all the Loves & Graces with them are Sin" (Ann. to Lavater, E590). And when Act becomes Crime, and the ornaments of perfection, envied horrors (see J. II: 28: 1–4, E172), restraint becomes virtue and is worshipped for its own sake as the cult of chastity—Thel's choice. Now all natural objects are clothed with prohibition, and no relationship is possible that is not tinged with a sense of criminality. Orc says of Albion to the Shadowy Female: "Jerusalem in his Garment & not thy Covering Cherub O lovely / Shadow of my delight who wanderest seeking for the prey" (M. I: 18: 37–38, E111). The Covering Cherub, the body of our accusations and denials, is the pre-existent layer of distance—perspectival distance, the distance of ritual and ceremony, and every other—which separates us from the things of perception, and its resonances extend far beyond conventions of sexuality. Its political implications are obvious; it is also the distance between mutually negating points of view. Confronting the Cherub everywhere, Albion's nightmare is one of perpetual Judgment, and the prisoner in the cavern is, at each impulse to freedom, condemned by his own threefold body: in Milton Percival's cogent formulation, his head is an Accuser, his heart a Judge, and his chaste loins an Executioner.[2]

We saw in chapter two how Albion's world falls from intimacy to hostile estrangement, how he enters a system of self-destruction in which he must struggle against nature to maintain a natural survival: "The corn is turn'd to thistles & the apples into poison" (J. I: 19: 10, E162). As the motif of externalization is developed through the three epics, it is increasingly presented in terms of accusation, until in *Jerusalem* Blake displays the terrors of Western history revolving around an agonized center of personal responsibility. At this core, a morality of the pure self emerges from the violent hatred with which Albion passes judgment on his emanation, his "unlawful pleasure":

> Phantom of the over heated brain! shadow of immortality!
> Seeking to keep my soul a victim to thy Love! which binds
> Man the enemy of man into deceitful friendships:
> Jerusalem is not! her daughters are indefinite:
> By demonstration, man alone can live, and not by faith.
> My mountains are my own, and I will keep them to myself.
> [J. I: 4: 24–29, E145]

Escaping from his shame at having loved Jerusalem, he conceals himself in the secret spaces of Vala's veil. Covered with boils, each a "separate & deadly Sin," he begs for a chaste natural body to literally hide his stain. His confusion is such that, even while he recognizes that his assumption of a new, cleaner form is a crucifixion of the Divine Body, his death lament reiterates his accusation, and his curse is necessarily directed both at the sinful object of his desire and, in his self-abhorrence, at himself: "O that Death & Annihilation were the same!" (21: 49, E165). With this suicidal despair, the critique of moral torment and purification that preoccupies Blake in *Thel, The Marriage,* and the *Visions of the Daughters of Albion* is fully revealed. The orthodoxy of vice and virtue openly converges with abstractionism in the end of humanity, as both self and other are sacrificed for the nourishment of imposed and reductive principles.

Blake's goal in *Jerusalem* is to wean us from an ethics of mutual negation to one of mutual forgiveness. As he presents it, forgiveness is less a moral principle contrary to accusation than a radical abandonment of moralism. Yet it involves more than a consideration of the object free from the encrustations and distortions of moralistic evaluation, for it is a positive movement of rapprochement, one that engages the senses in a growing perception of intimacy. The poem is dictated by the Saviour of Inspiration, who distinguishes himself from the remote God of Judgment:

> I am not a God afar off, I am a brother and friend;
> Within your bosoms I reside, and you reside in me:
> Lo! we are One; forgiving all Evil; Not seeking recompense!
> [J. I: 4: 18–20, E145]

In the frontispiece, Blake states the poem's theme of an unique and extreme kind of forgiveness, one that draws heavily on the Gospels but is ultimately Blake's own: "Half Friendship is the bitterest Enmity said Los / As he entered the Door of Death for Albions sake Inspired" (E143). The reason that it is Blake's own is that the agency of forgiveness, whose function is to bring back all that Albion has cast out, is the prophetic artist. Los's brotherhood is expressed neither by comforting the stricken Albion nor by turning the other cheek to the evils in which both are enmeshed, but by his excoriating attack on Albion's somnolence. Although his fury evokes hostility in the Cosmic Man, who commands his sons to seize the prophet, moderation would be half-friendship, an actual enmity that would keep the human form on its rock. In Los's work, sacrifice is transmuted, as, rather than surrendering his energy to an external God, he gives up his selfhood for the sake of man: "I am inspired: I act not for myself: for Albions sake / I now am what I am: a horror and an astonishment" (I: 8: 17–18, E150). Such a self-sacrifice must be understood as an integral part of Romantic enthusiasm. As the inspired Shelley is swept into the unifying power of the West Wind, as the inspired Keats journeys from himself into other bodies, so Los the prophet is subsumed into his Divine Work, leaving his natural self behind.

The paradigm of active forgiveness in the poem appears in the parable of Joseph and Mary, in which the final return of Jerusalem to Albion is prefigured. Like Marlowe, Blake believed that the Divine Child was simply illegitimate. But his purposes, more perhaps than Marlowe's, went beyond iconoclasm, for upon this conviction he creates a new myth in which Joseph's forgiveness of his wife's adultery determines the divinity of a child who, under the dispensation of moral severity, would be an outcast. The human act of forgiveness is thus Blake's Paraclete, an intervention of the imagination that opens the world within the center: "O point of mutual forgiveness between Enemies! / Birthplace of the Lamb of God incomprehensible!" (J. I: 7: 66–67, E149). At the end of the poem a new kind of Judgment is achieved, a Day of Wrath in which the principle of self-orientation is swept away and human friendship restored in its place. Albion arises to see Jesus appear as "Los my friend"; and the cosmic man's final entry into the furnaces is an act of self-sacrifice to save his friend from the threat of the approaching Cherub. In the regained Eden, everything is perceived in the human form of a friend: all men have become inspired. As the accused body leaves paradise, so the forgiven sources of man's joy—his sexual energy, his spontaneous openness to the promptings of inspiration, and his

direct knowledge of his own membership in Albion—return
him to it.

It is surprising on Plate 98 to see Locke, Newton, and
Bacon entering Eden together with Milton, Shakespeare, and
Chaucer, and the reader may be led at first to confuse forgiveness with charity. But to attribute moral generosity to the
poet at this point, as Hirsch does,[3] would be tantamount to
assigning Blake the power, St. Peter-like, of letting into Eden
those he chooses. In this case, Blake's renovation would merit
our dismissal as the phantom of an overheated brain, for it
would consist in the trade of one imperial clemency for another. On the contrary, Blake's Satanic Trinity enters Eden
simply because in his anti-elitist and anti-Calvinist paradise
all men are freed from their relative states and nothing is
holier than anything else. It is specifically a paradise where
Locke, with all other men, will live; for once Locke is liberated from the spectre who influenced his works his human
energy is no less Edenic than Milton's. Nor is Blake at the
end of *Jerusalem* finally sheathing his mental sword; forgiveness is not to be confused with acceptance or with intellectual
reconciliation. The spiritual wars of Eden are forgiving in
that they are cleansed of the conflict of selfhoods and based
on a common participation in Albion's unity. As Blake describes it, forgiveness does not diminish spiritual fury, but
concentrates it, transforming condemnation and retribution
into the strifes of imaginative creation.

Recovering the Appearances

Forgiveness is the perception of divine humanity in the
other. Los's labor of art is itself the substance of his forgiveness, and its theme is an expansion of our perceptual powers,
as well as a restoration of our full constitutive capacity. That
to imagine, as Los does, is to perceive with fullness and
clarity, is the theme of the following passage from *A Descriptive Catalogue:* "The Prophets describe what they saw in

Vision as real and existing men whom they saw with their imaginative and immortal organs; the Apostles the same; the clearer the organ the more distinct the object" (E532). The sensory multiplicity of the fallen body still survives in art, and the percepts of the poetic imagination, before they are subverted by rationalization, are still those of "immortal organs." Because of this, Blake says that we have not lost the potential to see both what and as the prophets saw, and, further, to come to live in what we see, as did the prophets, who were finally gathered into their vision.

The act of Los that is the foundation of his entire renovative work is the creation of the four States of Being: Ulro, Generation, Beulah, and Eden. Fisher calls a Blakean state of existence a "state of mind"; as a comparison, this is helpful because States of Being may change for Blakean man as easily and readily as mental or emotional states.[4] The difficulty, however, is in understanding Blake's literal contention that worlds, total fabrics of internal and external being, are as fluid and changeable as psychic states. The state of mind is instead the new way in which we are to see ourselves in relation to our condition. If we conceive of Generation, for example, as a stage of development, we are no longer *of* it, but rather *in* it at the moment: the man is primary to his situation, which is now but his present dwelling place. Through the creation of States Los gives man the context of free movement, which he requires to progress to Eden. The prophet's job is to remake our sense of the phenomenal world with art, to show us that our percepts come to us not absolutely but in relative appearances, as poems or paintings we have made. The cavern is not man's predestined structure, but one possible format of his perception which has been accepted as final; and Los must remove this sense of finality, humanize the environment by depicting it in its dependence upon the power of our senses. Redefining reality as a set of transmutable arrangements of mind, body, landscape, and experience, the invention of States is the recognition of a responsibility, both severe in its absoluteness and potentially liberating, in every human act, and upon this basis Los labors to increase perception until it can become simultaneous with creation.

I have discussed in the section on Error the reactive and merciful modes of creativity that produce Ulro and Generation. In *Milton* Blake gives considerable attention to a new stage of poetic consciousness that is not, by itself, apocalyptic, but that represents a first return of Los to authentic imagination. This is a work of consolation, of creating spaces for our sense of dissatisfaction with the world of reaction and mercy and for our hope of a new Golden Age. Art in this phase makes available to us the "inward form" of natural phenomena and experience, the pleasure and beauty within the center. In discovering for us a new opening to Upper Beulah, Los softens the divisions of Generation and the solitudes of Ulro and shows us places of refuge where we can know a sense of repose that is alien to the lower worlds. Here, also, a tear can become an intellectual thing and a sigh, the sword of an angel king (J. 52, E200), for these small acts of lamentation and yearning, when guarded and tempered by the prophet, can become instruments of renovation. For those of our feelings that cannot stand up to caverned credibility, Los builds in Beulah the Spaces of Erin, the political and geographical space of Ireland; such consolatory art is Albion's bulwark against the Atlantic floodwaters, and it is here that Jerusalem's shadow is sheltered in time of trouble. Through Los's increased efforts, Erin is developed into Dinah, a preliminary form of the restored Emanation, "Beautiful but terrible struggling to take a form of beauty" (III: 74: 53, E228). Our sense of possible beauty is intensified by Los until it is no longer willing to bear the restrictions of Generation, and the lamentations sheltered in Beulah are molded into a powerful sense of outrage, which seeks a confrontation with the forces of Satan and Rahab.

To create both Beulah and Eden Los must "open the im-

mortal Eyes / Of Man inwards into the Worlds of Thought"
(J. I: 5: 18–19, E146), or cultivate perception of those parts
of our experience which, not subject to empirical or analytical demonstration, are relegated to a ghost world of enter-
tainment or phantasy. The large task in *Jerusalem* is the
giving of bodily presence to a complete vision of reality that,
although unavailable to our "finite organical perception,"
was once known to the numerous senses of the ancient poets
and the "firm perswasion" of the Old Testament prophets
(see M.H.H.: 11–12, E37). Los's labor is intended to reorganize our perceptual powers beyond their given capacity
until we are able to know directly the Error that in the
spectral world of indistinctness and abstraction lacks sensory
immediacy for us; for the strategy of Satan is to remain
vague, and we "cannot behold him till he be reveald in his
System" (J. II: 43: 10, E189). But the fallen fragments claim,
"We are not One: we are Many" (I: 4: 23, E145); fallen
reason operates by the denial of relationship, in opposition to
the imagination, which, for the Romantics, is always a force
of connection.[5] Los reunifies the fragments of nature and of
fallen behavior by showing the ways in which they are related
to each other and to us, forcing them ultimately to unveil
themselves in either a human or an anti-human form.

Such a search for identities is the motivation of what has
been much analyzed as Blake's archetypal imagery: "The
stories of Arthur are the acts of Albion applied to a Prince
of the fifth century" (D.C., E534). Two points need to be
emphasized about the Blakean archetypes. The first is that
for Blake understanding such relationships is not sufficient;
we must actually see them, in the same way that Spenser's
Red Cross must actually see the true form of the witch
Duessa in order for her power over him to vanish. The
second is that the kind of reunification Blake has in mind is
not a mere dissolution of individuated form. Lack of distinctions, reductive standardization, what Blake calls vague and

cloudy general knowledge—these are the features of a world
that is only an accumulation of grains of sand. Rather, "all
men are alike (tho' infinitely various)" (A.R.O., E3). Oneness
for Blake is neither an idea nor an oceanic feeling, but a
sensory perception that must include a clear and minute
discrimination of individual character.

The mode of perception at work in Blake's imagery is, in
an epic extrapolation, that of the moment of heightened
consciousness around which later Romantic poems are built,
the visionary instant in which the divisions between inner
and outer, between symbol and letter, between subject and
object, and between objects themselves vanish and the lost
connections are suddenly recaptured. In such experiences
the veil of dualism is torn from the world to reveal a radical
unity, in which appearances are subject to a creative interchange between the perceiver and his environment. The
archetypes—or, as Wordsworth put it, the "Characters of the
Great Apocalypse"—are the forms of objects directly known
when perception, consciousness, and the world are suddenly
reintegrated. Within *Jerusalem* it is the job of Los to transform our images into such momentary visions, and his goal
is to give Albion not an insight or a theory but a direct perception of history and nature in the form of the Covering
Cherub.[6]

Just as he must clarify Error, Los must also realize a
sensory being for Truth. One way of describing the narrative
development of *Jerusalem* is as a progress in vision. The
poem recounts a slow and difficult opening of the doors of
perception, in which a paradigm of human knowledge, the
vision of the prophet, is finally attained by all men. The
signposts of this plot are the changing images that Blake uses
for the Divine Vision of Albion's wholeness and for Jerusalem.

When the senses narrow in the sacrifice of Luvah, the

Divine Vision shrinks away from man, and the mark of its distancing is its transformation into a Satanic parody of itself. The image of man's liberated completeness is metamorphosed through a series of appearances, from the bush and pillar of divine manifestation in Exodus, to the fiery cycle of destiny that binds man to the natural world, to the flaming sword of the Cherub, and finally to the punitive fires of Urizen's hell. But just as Luvah under the sacrificial knife splits into his parody, the body of violence, and his subterranean Orc form, so the Divine Vision remains itself in an exiled aspect, the globe of blood, which is the surviving humanity in our spaces, as the pulsation of an artery is in our times. The blood represents for Blake our lived experience of time and space, as well as that part of the matter and rhythm of man's natural life that is still a constant creation of his body.

Throughout *Jerusalem*, then, the Divine Vision always remains with Albion in its reduced form, as present and as close as the blood in his body. As an imminent possibility it is also perpetually available to him in its completeness, and beholding it, he would become it. But he flees from it repeatedly, choosing instead of his own Edenic identity its negation, or Satan.

The prophet is alone in his receptivity to the promptings of the Divine Vision, and, growing under his care, it slowly begins to emerge in flickering appearances within the world of nature. In the following image, one such appearance rescues Los from a despair that threatens to end his work:

> Also Los sick & terrified beheld the Furnaces of Death
> And must have died, but the Divine Saviour descended
> Among the infant loves & affections, and the Divine Vision
>   wept
> Like evening dew on every herb upon the breathing ground.
>   [J. II: 42: 5–8, E187]

This is, in some ways, a Wordsworthian moment in Blake's poetry: at a point of despondency and creative stasis for the poet, the things of nature are suddenly illuminated, shot through with a benevolent beauty, and the poet is reinspired through an unexpected communion with the landscape. But for Blake, this is far from a complete moment of vision. Such an appearance of the Divine Vision is valued as encouragement for the laboring prophet and as a promise of what might come, and the weeping affections are only the delicate beginnings of renewal. One plate later, however, Blake goes beyond the naturalistic vision:

> Then the Divine Vision like a silent Sun appeard above
> Albions dark rocks: setting behind the Gardens of Kensington
> On Tyburns River, in clouds of blood: where was mild Zion Hills
> Most ancient promontory, and in the Sun, a Human Form appeard
> And thus the Voice Divine went forth upon the rocks of Albion.   [43: 1–5, E189]

The approach of the perceived in the first passage is suggested by its assumption of human characteristics: it enters into relation with man, it seems to communicate with him. But now nature assumes complete human form, and it speaks literally and directly. The return of the landscape first to a state that seems both human and natural at the same time, a luminous mid-world of mutuality, and then to a fully human state is repeated in the final stages of Albion's awakening. Albion rises when the Divine Vision is brought close enough to him to be felt as a breath: the same kind of exhalation—like a breeze and like the breath of another person, except that it is larger than any single person—that attracts Wordsworth, Coleridge, and Shelley. Here, the Divine Vision is experienced as a premonition of humanity in the world of objects. To Albion's fully aroused senses, it emerges in the human form of another man. And when Albion enters the furnaces, the Divine Vision, like Jerusalem, disappears from the poem as a discrete image, for Albion, as perceiver, becomes him, as everything he perceives becomes Jerusalem.

The images of Jerusalem follow the same pattern of an exile, a split into a parody and a diminished form, and then a gradual re-emergence through the work of Los; although, like Ololon and Asia, Jerusalem must also pass through a separate process of education before she can accept a final return. In her original state, the emanation is perceived as the radiance that characterizes the objects of Edenic perception, for she is the translucency within the center; but after the fall, she becomes opaque and vague, "scattered abroad like a cloud of smoke thro' non-entity" (J. I: 5: 13, E146). The veil of her parody, Vala, is precisely this obscurity of the desired. It can be said that Los's task of vision is to see what it is that Albion really wants. Jerusalem and Vala are the true and false brides, and as the cosmic man, turning outward, is increasingly attracted to the idolized form of his desire, Jerusalem fades before her rival in his eyes, just as the Divine Vision does before the Spectre.[7] When Vala is "raised up as Mother! Nature!" the appearances of Jerusalem are divided in two motifs of imagery. In the first she becomes a Shadow of Eternal Delight in Beulah, where she remains available to fallen man in a limited form as physical and mental play, sex and art as we know them. But her joys, subversive of Vala's dominance, come under increasingly violent denunciation, and in the second motif Jerusalem is depicted as "the impurity and the harlot," a slave at Vala's Spindle of Destruction, her sense of her own identity so obliterated by her rival's accusations that she has become mad with self-indictment and defaces herself into the form Vala would have her assume.

It is then, in the Dungeons of Babylon, that the "insane" and "inarticulate" Jerusalem "faintly" sees the Divine Vision.

But the revelation at the nadir almost passes her by, for, under the spell of five-sense cognition, she hesitates before the undemonstrable Divine Appearance of man, just as she has lost the conviction of her own Divine Appearance:

> Art thou alive! & livest thou for-evermore? or art thou
> Not: but a delusive shadow, a thought that liveth not.
> Babel mocks saying, there is no God nor Son of God
> That thou O Human Imagination, O Divine Body art all
> A delusion. but I know thee O Lord when thou arisest upon
> My weary eyes even in this dungeon & this iron mill.
>
> [III: 60: 54–59, E209]

During their interview, the Divine Vision begins the renewal of Jerusalem by rebuilding her sense of the holiness of her own body. She learns, first, through the parable of Joseph and Mary, to separate the spontaneous enactment of desire from the imputation of sin. Second, she is taught that her body is primary to any of its states of being, a startling kind of primacy to be realized at the Awakening: "Man in the Resurrection changes his Sexual Garments at Will / Every Harlot was once a Virgin: every Criminal an Infant Love!" (61: 51–52, E210). And third, she is persuaded to trust in the reality of inspiration even while she must continue in a world of demonstration:

> But I thy Magdalen behold thy Spiritual Risen Body
> Shall Albion arise? I know he shall arise at the Last Day!
> I know that in my flesh I shall see God.   [62: 14–16, E211]

Now, prepared for the prospect of a reunion with human consciousness, she must endure further exile until Los can re-create her lost form, for the emanation is the created and cannot bring anything about, not even to the extent of changing her own debased appearance.

Los develops two visions of Jerusalem. In the first, he sees that the city of Eden has become the desert of Ulro: "Naked Jerusalem lay before the Gates upon Mount Zion / The Hill

of Giants, all her foundations levelld with the dust!" (see IV:
78: 10–29, E231). This is a turning point in Los's work, for if
the lost emanation is still within the things of the world, even
in a ruined and fragmented form, then renewal must necessarily be a reorganization of the given, and to leave the world
in will, desire, or imagination would be to close off the promise of Eden once and for all. Blake's exuberant faith in renovation depends upon a conviction that the banished appearances of paradise continue to exist in the fallen world. The
imagination is outside us, hidden in the landscape, as it is
also hidden within our natural minds and perceptual organs,
and it speaks to the prophetic senses from the outside we all
see. Incapable of being annihilated, Jerusalem, like the Divine Vision, always remains with us in transmuted appearances according to our transmuted perceptual powers, and
the form and clarity of her presence at any given moment
directly reflects our condition.

In the second vision, Los unveils Jerusalem's lost completeness:

> I see thy Form O lovely mild Jerusalem, Wingd with Six
>   Wings
> In the opacous Bosom of the Sleeper, lovely Three-fold
> In Head & Heart & Reins three Universes of love & beauty
> Thy forehead bright: Holiness to the Lord, with Gates of
>   pearl
> Reflects Eternity beneath thy azure wings of feathery down
> Ribbd delicate & clothd with featherd gold & azure & purple
>   .   .   .   .   .
> I see the New Jerusalem descending out of Heaven
> Between thy Wings of gold & silver featherd immortal
> Clear as the rainbow, as the cloud of the Suns tabernacle
>
> Thy Reins coverd with Wings translucent sometimes covering
> And sometimes spread abroad reveal the flames of holiness
> Which like a robe covers: & like a Veil of Seraphim
> In flaming fire unceasing burns from Eternity to Eternity.
>   [86: 1–25, E242]

The vision of Jerusalem is radically non-perspectival; she is like the transfigured Asia, whose radiance and abundance overflows images and whose "limbs are burning / Through the vest which seems to hide them" (*Prometheus Unbound* II: v: 54–55). To the natural eye, Jerusalem has no recognizable form; she is neither woman nor city but both at the same time. Yet the sense of hearing is equipped to move with better comprehension from one to another of the images of sexuality and environment that compose her appearance. And Blake reinforces her aural framing with a slight detail: "Bells of silver round thy knees living articulate / Comforting sounds of love & harmony" (29–30).

I have emphasized in this chapter that the function of art in Blake is to return the fullness of the world to our senses; but in order for this to be possible the senses themselves need to undergo significant alteration. To understand this process and to understand, as well, why Los's final vision of the Emanation departs from perspectivism in a specific manner, we must turn to a consideration of the ways in which the particular senses are engaged and transformed in the work of renewal.

The Senses

Hearing and Speaking

"Poetry Painting & Music the three Powers (in Man) of conversing with Paradise which the flood did not Sweep away" (V.L.J., E548).

It is not incidental that Blake speaks of "conversing" with paradise through art, even in reference to the visual art of painting, for, relatively free from the perspectival conditions of viewpoint, direction, and horizon, the sense of hearing suggests the liberty of the imagination. Thus, before the fall, the Edenic earth in which Urthona propagated his emanations was not natural soil but "the Auricular Nerves of

Human life" (F.Z. I: 4: 1, E297). And a frequent image for
the falling away from man of the objects of perception is the
muting of nature's voices: "A Rock a Cloud a Mountain /
Were now not Vocal as in Climes of happy Eternity" (VI:
71a: 4–5, E341). The natural ear is no less enclosed and externalized than the eye, and its whorled form images the
vortex of fallen perception: "a whirlpool fierce to draw creations in" (B.T.: 6: 17, E6). Yet it remains an organ of nexus
with the world from which we have fallen, and its spiral is
described as upwards, rather than downwards, in its projec-
tion: "A golden ascent winding round to the heavens of
heavens" (F.Z., VI: 73: 38, E343).

Because of the ear's privilege, Blake describes poetic inspiration as an act of hearing a voice. The closed system of
the visible world is too poor to produce a seed or a poem;
nor can a poem be willed. The work of art is a bridge between the given and Eden, and its source is a visitation
through the sense of hearing from outside the system of
natural experience. Blake is not being merely decorative,
then, when he tells us that *Europe* is dictated to him by a
fairy, or *Jerusalem* by the Divine Vision. The theme appears,
rather more strikingly, in his correspondence. In a letter to
Butts, in which he describes writing *Jerusalem* from "immediate Dictation" and sometimes "even against my Will,"
he claims that he often has visions and dreams in which he
converses with friends in Eternity (Apr. 25, 1803, E697). And,
in a letter to Hayley, he claims to speak daily and hourly with
his dead brother: "I hear his advice & even now write from
his Dictate" (May 6, 1800, E678).

In these situations the poet is awakened to new vision;
and it is always important to distinguish the awakenings in
Blake which are simply openings of the eyes from those in
which the eyes are opened as a result of a voice. The first
kind refers to the fall into nature, as in the division of
Tharmas and Enion. The second kind refers to situations of

renovation or of revolutionary disturbance. In *Europe,* for
instance, the voice of Orc awakens Los and impels him to join
in the "strife of blood." And Albion's "clay cold ear" is
pierced by the voice of Britannia at his final rising. In exactly the same way, the poet is aroused by the Divine Vision
at the outset of *Jerusalem:*

> This theme calls me in sleep night after night, & ev'ry morn
> Awakes me at sun-rise, then I see the Saviour over me
> Spreading his beams of love, & dictating the words of this
>   mild song.
>
> Awake! awake O sleeper of the land of shadows, wake!
>   expand! [I: 4: 3–6, E145]

At the end of the poem, then, Albion is inspired; he too becomes a poet.

Perception is cleansed through a shift to the mode of another sense organ than the eye, and the recurrent dramatic
moment of a voice cutting into "single vision and Newton's
sleep" suggests that the ear is the most powerful agency for
breaking the spell of the visual. It is not enough for us to
find different ways of seeing, or to see more intensely; we
must learn to use the sense of hearing as we presently use
sight, to *see* with the ear. The strange letter referring to the
conversations with Robert Blake might tempt a reader to
reach for his Swedenborg; but Book XIV of *The Prelude,*
in which Wordsworth writes of the "glorious faculty" of
"higher minds," is much more to the point:

>   in a world of life they live,
> By sensible impressions not enthralled,
> But by their quickening impulse made more prompt
> To hold fit converse with the spiritual world,
> And with the generations of mankind
> Spread over time, past, present, and to come,
> Age after age, till Time shall be no more. [105–11] [8]

"Fit converse" is an apt description of the visionary experience in Blake. The sound that wakes is most often that of
speech. The "auricular nerves," the ground of verbal communication, are socializing, rather than individuating as
the perspectival eye is, and are thus appropriately pivotal
to a myth of reintegration. Indeed, the visionary Los is not
exactly one who sees what others cannot see—the Divine
Vision, Jerusalem, the Covering Cherub—but one who ar-
ticulates these unseen presences, speaks them to the rest of us,
and teaches us to perceive them with his words. His final
"visions" in *Jerusalem* of the Cherub and the Emanation are
more accurately poetic verbalizations, spoken descriptions of
imaginative appearances unavailable to the perspectival eye,
and they represent the culmination of a progress of revolutionary utterance that has its first stirrings in the howls and
outcries of the animals in "Auguries of Innocence" and the
roaring of Rintrah in *The Marriage*. What Frye has called
the visualization of the desired seems to have less to do with
the eye than with the voice; and the poet's job of illumination appears to be one of converting visual forms to auditory.
So the guinea-sun of ordinary perception appears to the visionary as a chorus of angels singing, "Holy Holy Holy"; and
Los creates the sunrise of the Judgment Day "in the ear":
"Look how the opening dawn advances with vocal harmony"
(F.Z. IX: 127: 3, E381).

Visualizing differs from seeing in that it entails the active
participation of the perceiver; but what represents most fully
for Blake the body's constitutive engagement in phenomena
is the act of utterance. All speech, to a varying degree, involves
a task of formulation, and this is, of course, most of all so in
the rigors of poetic speech. But, more than this, Blake believes that our words create and sustain our world and that
they have, as well, the capability to change it. Vocalization is
so powerful a force in Blake that spoken words become as
directly instrumental as tools or physical actions. Thus, when
Albion curses Jerusalem, humanity, and himself, he immedi-

ately falls into the World of Death: "What have I said? What
have I done? O all-powerful Human Words! / You recoil
back upon me in the blood of the Lamb slain in his Children" (J. I: 24: 1–2, E167). The result of his curse is described in a physical image—"Thundering the Veil rushes
from his hand Vegetating Knot by / Knot, Day by Day, Night
by Night" (61–62, E169)—the synesthetic effects of which are
so complex as to disguise at first the fact that Blake is speaking of the body and its powers, intimating that compartmentalized five-sense perception cannot tell us how spoken words
can bear the visible world as their issue, how something
spoken is also something physically made and therefore thun-
ders from the hand. The power of speech is also figured recur-
rently as a creative wind, or breath of prophetic utterance.
Sometimes it would sweep through the landscape and destroy
it; in the following lyric the speaker retreats from his own
prophetic impulse and consequently creates the barrens of
Ulro:

> I feard the fury of my wind
> Would blight all blossoms fair & true
> And my sun it shind & shind
> And my wind it never blew
>
> But a blossom fair or true
> Was not found on any tree
> For all blossoms grew & grew
> Fruitless false tho fair to see.   [E458]

Sometimes the wind is mild and fertilizing: at the end of
The Four Zoas Luvah returns to Vala as a "vocal wind," in
which "her garments rejoice," and a "creating voice" that
wakes "the Soul from its grassy bed" (see IX: 126: 30–127:
6, E380). In *Jerusalem*, Los's physical acts of vocalization,
bardic song and prophetic utterance, are creative organiza-
tions of real phenomena, and to "speak" the appearances as
he does is to call them into effective being.

The association of the ear and paradise and the centrality

of a passage from seeing with the eye to seeing with the ear are crucial motifs in Romantic and post-Romantic verse. Wordsworth, in natural contexts, usually bases his visionary descriptions on this shift, which in such lyrics as "The Green Linnet" and "To the Cuckoo," prototypes of the Romantic poem on the singing of birds, becomes a primary dramatic event in itself. In "To the Cuckoo" the bird's song takes the poet back to a period in his life before the self knew estrangement from the landscape:

> And I can listen to thee yet;
> Can lie upon the plain
> And listen, till I do beget
> That golden time again.

The auditory is used to dissolve the compartments and horizons of the mature eye, to counter the feeling of mortality and the sharpened awareness of vanishing that arise from a visually based sense of individuation. Blake is explicit about the association of death and the eye: "But in the Optic vegetative Nerves Sleep was transformed / To Death in old time by Satan the father of Sin & Death" (M. I: 29: 32–33, E126). But the time of the ear is not that of the eye; Blake writes to Butts that the duration of writing *Jerusalem,* the time of auditory dictation by a non-visual spirit, was "renderd Non Existent" (Apr. 25, 1803, E697). Similarly, Shelley has a remarkable auditory figure for redeemed time in Act IV of *Prometheus Unbound.* In the song and dance of the Chorus of Hours, the temporality of clock and calendar is replaced by that of rhythm and choreography. The implication is that time is now at the disposition of the perceiver, a music-maker, who, rather than submitting to its compartments, organizes it according to his impulses.

The struggle of the poetic voice against death is nowhere richer and more intricate than in the *Duino Elegies.* In "The Ninth Elegy," Rilke exhorts us to "speak and proclaim" the "things that live on departure":

> fleeting, they look for
> rescue through something in us, the most fleeting of all.
> Want us to change them entirely, within our invisible hearts,
> into—oh, endlessly—into ourselves! Whosoever we are.
>
> Earth, isn't this what you want: an invisible
> re-arising in us? Is it not your dream
> to be one day invisible? Earth! invisible!
> What is your urgent command, if not transformation? [9]

The things of nature that vanish from the spectator's field rearise in the imagination, as poetic speech rather than visibilia, and this is to be understood as a metamorphosis of one kind of matter into another. In "The Tenth Elegy," freed from spectatorship and from the fear of non-existence, the youthful visitor to the Landscape of Lamentation, with the help of his female guide, discovers a changed perception: the complete figure of being, on the double page of life and death, is seen by the ear. Together they stand before the Sphinx:

> His sight, still dizzy with early death,
> can't take it in. But her gaze
> frightens an owl from behind the pschent. And the bird,
> brushing, in slow neat-quitting, along the cheek,
> the one with the ripest curve,
> faintly inscribes on the new
> death-born hearing, as though on the double
> page of an opened book, the indescribable outline. [10]

"The Tenth Elegy" is closer in spirit to the Keats of "Melancholy" and "Autumn" than to Blake, but it can help us understand *Jerusalem* and, in particular, the nature of Los's work. It is to counter the vanishings of the eye that Los builds his city of art, Golgonooza:

> I in Six Thousand Years walk up and down: for not one
> Moment
> Of Time is lost, nor one Event of Space unpermanent.

> But all remain: every fabric of Six Thousand Years
> Remains permanent: tho' on the Earth where Satan
> Fell, and was cut off all things vanish & are seen no more
> They vanish not from me & mine, we guard them first &
>   last[.]
> The generations of men run on in the tide of Time
> But leave their destind lineaments permanent for ever & ever.
>   [M. I: 22: 18–25, E116]

Blake suggests a new sense of reality, not abstracted from sight but created by human speech, and, as we have seen, the act of speech in its widest sense comprehends all forms of art. In the furnaces of Los, phenomena undergo the passage from eye to ear; there, not subject to visual limitations, they can unfold to their fullest forms. When finally Albion commits himself to the fires, the Covering Cherub, the summary of our visibilia, disappears like a dream, and the world itself rearises—invisibly to the perspectival eye—as the resurrected body of man, alive once again in the "golden time." And when Jerusalem is finally released in the vanishing of all objects of the natural eye, she is perceived in the cries of the renovated human forms. As first only Los could articulate her, now all can. The struggle toward vision is accomplished: all men have realized their prophetic faculties. Now there is no perspectival imagery of any kind, but simply the joyful crying of her name, and she surrounds the perceiver like a sound.

An Auditory Style

The shift from eye to ear tells us not only about the process of renewal, but also about the workings of Blake's style, for his verse reveals a strikingly aural bias. The evolution of his technique suggests, indeed, that he is concerned not only with bringing qualities of the spoken voice back into poetry and thereby re-establishing verse as a specifically auditory art form, but, further, with developing an expressive mode organized according to the ways in which the ear, in radical contrast to the eye, structures information. It is upon this distinction that he bases an elaborate visionary poetics.

That his early lyric poetry is grounded in the traditional oral modes of song and ballad is only the initial sign of his interest, for his poetic world, in its completeness, is largely one of sounds and voices. His landscapes are generally unrecognizable to the eye; often, as in *The Book of Urizen*, he presents us with a sequence of fire, darkness, and whirl-winds that defies visualization:

> His cold horrors silent, dark Urizen
> Prepar'd: his ten thousands of thunders
> Rang'd in gloom'd array stretch out across
> The dread world, & the rolling of wheels
> As of swelling seas, sound in his clouds
> In his hills of stor'd snows, in his mountains
> Of hail & ice; voices of terror,
> Are heard, like thunders of autumn
> When the cloud blazes over the harvests.   [3: 27–35, E70]

Often the visible aspect of the image moves too quickly for the naturalistic eye to follow. The following image of Albion's naturalization, if presented by stages rather than in a single sweep, might not disturb the eye as much as it does:

> Cold snows drifted around him: ice coverd his loins around
> He sat by Tyburns brook, and underneath his heel, shot up!
> A deadly Tree, he nam'd it Moral Virtue, and the Law
> Of God who dwells in Chaos hidden from the human sight.
> The Tree spread over him its cold shadows (Albion groand)
> They bent down, they felt the earth and again enrooting
> Shot into many a Tree! an endless labyrinth of woe!
> [J. II: 28: 13–19, E172]

And often the components of an image will singly offer the eye no difficulty, but their interrelations and the transi-

tions from one to another cannot be reconciled with the eye's
experience or expectation:

> And a roof, vast petrific around,
> On all sides He fram'd: like a womb;
> Where thousands of rivers in veins
> Of blood pour down the mountains to cool
> The eternal fires beating without
> From Eternals; & like a black globe
> View'd by sons of Eternity, standing
> On the shore of the infinite ocean
> Like a human heart strugling & beating
> The vast world of Urizen appear'd.   [B.U.: 5: 28–37, E72]

Furthermore, by setting this scene—and most of his poetry—
among "Eternals," Blake implicitly tells us that what he
shows is like nothing we have ever seen and nothing we are
able to see with our present powers of sight. Blake strains
the eye, and, by doing so, he forces us to shift to the ear,
to try to hear the image. Sometimes, when describing a visual
scene, he does so as if he were relating to us a picture he
knew we could not see:

> Then Albion drew England into his bosom in groans & tears
> But she stretched out her starry Night in Spaces against him.
>   like
> A long Serpent, in the Abyss of the Spectre which augmented
> The Night with Dragon wings coverd with stars & in the
>   Wings
> Jerusalem & Vala appeared: & above between the Wings mag-
>   nificent
> The Divine Vision dimly appear'd in clouds of blood weep-
>   ing.   [J. III: 54: 27–32, E202]

Blake seems to be saying, "Over here is . . . over there is
. . . above is . . ." This is a picture as it is filtered through
the sense of hearing. We are given no sense of the frame,
horizon, or viewpoint which a naturalistically perceived
visual scene would have, but instead a sense of the por-

tions of the picture as they appear purely in relationship to
each other. Such a field of unframed and ungrounded interrelations is the space evoked by myth, dream, and religious
vision, in which the figures and events seem free-floating in
some other world than our own—i.e., another than that of
the eye. Nor is there any sense of empty space in Blake's
auditory picture. Such space does not matter to the ear;
it is concerned with *space as it is filled,* while the naturalistic
eye is concerned with *space to be filled,* and therefore susceptible of empty spots, or voids.

Jean Hagstrum writes that "Blake's verse is sometimes
baffling because he carries to extreme what has elsewhere
been called the picture-gallery technique of ordering poetic
materials—one moves from painting to painting as in a room.
Contiguity replaces narration." [11] But the more one forces
visual analogues on Blake's style, the more baffling it becomes. The contiguity is, in fact, one of dramatic voices,
rather than pictures. Much misinterpretation of Blake is due
to an attempt to read him with the eye, instead of the ear.
As a poet interested in voice, Blake would subscribe to Whit-
man's "Each existence has its own idiom," [12] and this applies
to both matter and manner. But Blake, more than most poets
of the voice, conveys meaning through the latter, the tone of
an utterance; and interpretation which ignores this is in
danger of becoming mistracked from the beginning. Thus,
"The Tyger" (S.E., E24), when read purely with the eye,
appears as a powerful apprehension of supernatural force,
possibly of evil, possibly of prophetic wrath, and the tiger is
then an emblem of God's capacity for evil or of Christ the
Tiger. But the poem is spoken in awe, dread, questioning,
and astonishment, and this tonality is never used by Blake to
represent a state of complete perception. Blake's prophetic
voice, the one he uses, for instance, in "To Tirzah" or in the
prose, where he is not speaking through dramatic characters,
is one of exultant conviction. There is nothing of dread in

his voice, because there is nothing he holds in dread. Every-thing that lives is holy, and there is nothing in Blake's reality to fear or bow down before. Blake's Jesus is one's own humanity, and to think of revolutionary energy as something apart from one's own body and imagination and those of other men—and particularly to think of energy as animal rather than human—is precisely the kind of displacement Blake sets out to correct. The speaker of "The Tyger" is rather like Job when he wonders about the terrors of God which "set themselves in array against me" (6 : 4). Catching the tone of a dramatic voice in Blake is perhaps a surer guide to rudimentary understanding than a frontal assault on the symbology. Given the particular voice of the poem, it be-comes clear that the forests of night are Entuthon-Benython, the forests of illusion, the depths of the caverned mind in which energy appears demonic and Urizen frightens us to his altars by showing us monsters. And it also becomes highly probable that the poem's tiger is not the tiger of wrath who is wiser than the horse of instruction, but another Blakean tiger, the one in *The Four Zoas* who "laughs at the Human form" (I: 15: 2, E304), whose power and beauty are a terrifying mockery of man's smallness. The tiger visualized by the poem's dramatic speaker is a product of incomplete percep-tion; it is a phantasy, a delusion. The imaginative posture Blake delineates in this poem is clearly heard in the manner of its utterance.[13]

Similarly, it is difficult to understand how the world por-trayed in the *Songs of Innocence* could possibly be idealized in commentary, when the tonality of these poems is so dominantly one of fear, weeping, lamentation, and calling for help. Innocence, as Blake describes it, is no paradise of the unborn, but the world of childhood, apprehended most often in the moment of its transformation into something else. Innocence, in many of these poems, is already behind the speaker. "The Ecchoing Green" (E8), for instance, is a poem of initiation into the vanishings of natural time and space. In "The Little Black Boy" (E9) and "The Chimney Sweeper" (E10), poems of great sadness, the speakers are quietly consigned to the depths of the cavern as they naively accept the rationalizations of their oppressors. And before its break-up, Innocence is a delicate world of trust and benignity ever in danger of collapsing into tears and fright. Blake has the dramatist's skill of making all his voices convincing. All his speakers suffer the pains of the fall, and all talk about renewal; but no matter how taken in one is by the sense or the depth of feeling or the poetic beauty of, say, Urizen's great lament in Night V (63: 23–65: 12, E336), the tone of lamentation indicates that what he says must be fallacious or villainous or, at best (and not in this case), well-intentioned but only partly perceptive.

Blake's technique of the dramatic voice reaches its most sophisticated development in the epics, and perhaps especially in *The Four Zoas*.[14] In this poem, we are given no consistent authorial voice to serve as a norm by which to gauge the dramatic speakers. We are thrown in among a series of speeches by characters who compete for our sympathies by the force and beauty of their utterances, each trying to persuade us that only he or she is correct in his interpretations, assumptions, and programs. Action and landscape are filtered through their viewpoints, and events are given to us in multiple conflicting versions. When Albion's integrity is usurped by the selfhoods of his now autonomous components, each fragment sees the whole according to his own part and tries in this way to become a Divine Tyrant. By juxtaposing these viewpoints against one another and by surrounding the dramatic speeches with images of blindness, fancy, and delusion, Blake shows the inadequacy of any one of the perspectives. At root this is a technique of satire, and the early *An Island in the Moon,* in which Blake employs it with a tone of conventional satiric mockery, is in the tradition of *Bartholomew Fair*, *The Dunciad*, and *A Tale of a Tub*. But Blake's anti-perspectivism differs crucially from that of Jonson, Pope, and Swift, because, where they show the inadequacy of particular perspectives, Blake satirizes perspectivism itself. In *The Four Zoas*, every being has, and is, his own truth, every being is petrified into his own point of view, and every point of view is a negation of every other. Perspectivism is the sight of the selfhood, the Urizenic eye which seeks repose in a zenith from which all can be viewed within the guidelines of the limiting compass, as in "The Ancient of Days." Even in Night IX Urizen is thinking delusively, when he asks: "Where shall we take our stand to view the infinite & unbounded / Or where are human feet for Lo our eyes are in the heavens" (122: 24–25, E377). The infinite cannot be viewed from a set physical position, because the feeling of infinity depends upon the absence of perspective.

Related to Blake's anti-perspectivism is a technique of multi-perspectivism which is used with particular concentration in Night VIII, as Blake insistently gives close and distant prospects of single phenomena: "Mystery / When viewd remote She is One when viewd near she divides / To multitude" (105: 15–17, E364). Elsewhere, as we have seen, multi-perspectivism is used not as a narrative device, but as an image for the flexible Edenic eye which is not limited to a single viewpoint upon a given object. A particularly complex kind of multi-perspectivism is sometimes employed in depicting images of motion, most remarkably that of Milton's descent through the vortex and his fall into the natural world. If we return to that sequence, we find Blake using a moving focus to portray what Milton sees as he falls first into a zenith perspective upon Albion and finally into Albion's body on the earth, from which he looks up at the "cloudy heaven" of his original viewpoint. Next, Blake shifts to an authorial perspective of Milton's shadow falling into the Sea of Time and Space, and then to the viewpoint of himself, as a character on earth, watching Milton's descent as a falling star. Later, the track of Milton's fall becomes a moving viewpoint for Ololon to follow; her voyage, in fact, is described as a voyage of the eye, a downward visual swoop through a series of perspectives, rather than a veritable physical flight like Milton's (II: 34: 1–35: 41, E132–35).

The prevalence of such images in *Milton* may be due to a similar kind of visual imagery recurrent in *Paradise Lost*. Describing Satan's flight to the Gates of Hell, Milton shifts from Satan's moving viewpoint to his distant appearance as a merchant fleet when seen from the Gates, and then shifts back to Satan's perspective as he closes in on his destination (II: 629–48). And, in another image, he describes the approach of Satan's forces, as follows:

> at last
> Far in th' Horizon to the North appear'd
> From skirt to skirt a fiery Region, stretcht
> In battailous aspect, and nearer view
> Bristl'd with upright beams innumerable
> Of rigid Spears, and Helmets throng'd, and Shields
> Various, with boastful Argument portray'd,
> The banded Powers of *Satan* hasting on
> With furious expedition.[15]

Sergei Eisenstein cites this passage for its anticipation of the montage possibilities of film.[16] But Milton's image differs from, say, Eisenstein's brilliant depiction of the armies approaching over the ice in *Alexander Nevsky* in that, while in the latter we see an ominous blur on the horizon become a throng of rushing soldiers, in Milton a fiery region becomes an army, or a fleet becomes Satan. The difference is that of a clarification of something difficult to make out as opposed to a transformation of one thing into another. There are really two perspectives in the Milton image, one gliding into the other; there is only one, however well elaborated, in the

Eisenstein. Blake's use of the technique is more complex than
Milton's, because he does not use a simile for his distant
view. While Milton would say that Satan viewed afar looks
like a fleet, Blake says that Mystery viewed afar *is* the Great
Whore Babylon. Ultimately Milton regards the distant appearance as esthetically and dramatically powerful, but fallacious. But in Blake both images of Mystery are equally
veridical, for the point of view determines the object's identity. It is as we see it; and "As a man is So he Sees" (Letter
to Dr. Trusler, Aug. 23, 1799, E677). Furthermore, while in
Milton the perspectives are consecutive, in Blake they are
essentially simultaneous. Blake says that if we look from this
viewpoint and if we look from that viewpoint, the object
will appear first so, then so. To freeze the object into either
one of these perspectives is to idolize it and to lose direct
knowledge of its full reality. An eye capable of multiple perspectives at any given moment is radically unlike the bodily
eye we have. That eye can see what Eisenstein sees; it can
see *as,* but not *what,* Milton sees; it can see neither as nor
what Blake sees.

An image resembling in structure that of Milton's fall,
moreover, is probably unfilmable because the perspectival
shift is a reversal which occurs in what is essentially one
sweeping syntactical movement:

> Hovering over the cold bosom, in its vortex Milton bent
> down
> To the bosom of death, what was underneath soon seemd
> above.
> A cloudy heaven mingled with stormy seas in loudest ruin.
>
> [I: 15: 41–43]

For least artificial cinematic results, a similarly structured
image would probably have to be cut into two shots, and
the all-important rhythm of the reversal would be lost. Film
is by no means limited to the possibilities of natural sight,

but Blake is developing a movement of the eye which, even 150 years later, is unavailable to any procedure of visual representation we have. Yet it is demonstrably a movement available to the creative powers of the speaking voice and the receptive powers of the ear. Blake is, again, forcing the reader from eye to ear in order to see.

Blake's use of the special possibilities of voice and ear to create poetic meaning is also evident in the more properly sonic phase of his verse, in his prosody and in the sheer sound and rhythms of his language. This is particularly noticeable when he is working in the fourteener. Frye has written of a mode of satiric language which is characterized by the "verbal tempest," a linguistic giantism expressed in waves of language and in such forms as the catalogue.[17] He mentions Isaiah, Rabelais, Swift, and Joyce as masters of this style, and Blake might well be mentioned too. But in Blake's epics an exuberent rhythmic and verbal energy is played off against a dramatic context. Blake's point is that the energy is misdirected, poured into the curses and laments of the characters, into descriptions of their gigantic turmoils and agonized labors, and into their mutually negating arguments and their soliloquizing. Dramatically, this is energy desperately seeking a satisfactory verbal form, and too often finding its outlet in monologue, the form of speech most appropriate to a state of unrelated selfhood. But the auditory frame of the fourteener adds another dimension to Blake's sound. John Hollander has suggested that Blake was highly conscious of the emblematic potentialities of meter, how it can engage conventions and traditions and become a significative aspect of the utterance.[18] Thus, we might say, while language and rhythm assert the fury of the fallen characters, the special rhythmic character of the long line and its recurrent ictus assert another kind of fury, that of the prophetic cadence of the Old Testament—and, as Hollander observes, of a Miltonic cadence which, to Blake's ear, had been diluted out of eighteenth-century iambic pentameter and was now recognizable only in a longer line. It is not until the Edenic vision at the end of *Jerusalem* that the characters in that poem greet each other and actually converse. Until Eden that confrontation can only take place through the poet's craft which, literally, organizes fallen utterance into prophetic rhythm; and which, considering that utterance as contrary rather than negation, metrically carries out the encounter which is refused by the accusing and soliloquizing voices.

Another aspect of Blake's sound, one that closely links him to the later Romantics, is his striving for a "common speech" —i.e., an oral, rather than literary, poetic effect. Frye writes: "Blake's Prophetic Books represent one of the few successful efforts to tackle conversational rhythm in verse—so successful that many critics are still wondering if they are 'real poetry.' Blake's view [was] that a longer line than the pentameter was needed to represent educated colloquial speech in verse." [19] We need to remember, however, that Blake's idea of educated informal discourse differs from ours, and that to him Isaiah and Ezekiel, his dinner guests in *The Marriage of Heaven and Hell,* were the masters of educated conversation. For Blake the true speech of the common man is the speech of oracular utterance. Hollander and S. Foster Damon have noted, further, that Blake's handling of meter is strongly geared to an oral effect; Hollander comments that the general "principle of his free accentualism throughout his work has been to let speech stress, in its syntactic and rhetorical context, govern the metrical role of the syllables." [20] The observation might be applied as well to Blake's syntax, in which the structure and sequence of phrases is determined by vocal emphases, the rhythms of conjunction and strategic repetition, and the dramatic interplay of question and assertion, invocation and exclamation. It is also possible that Blake's punctuation is not purely eccentric, but suggestive of an attempt to capture more precisely the tonality and rhythm of oral utterance by using comma, period, colon, and semicolon (as well as the line-break) to indicate varying degrees of caesura. Francis Berry, in showing that it is through "the totality of printed signs on the page that the poet conveys his voice," reminds us of the "eccentric" punctuation of Shakespeare and Milton, two writers with a strongly oral bias.[21]

There are other stylistic traits that give Blake's late work a quasi-musical impact. One instance is his use of tag-lines, generally with variation, such as those dealing with the flashes of Divine Vision, the thundering of Los's bellows and the blast of his furnaces, and the repose of Albion on his rocks. These are more intricate devices than refrains, because they summarize and evoke enormously comprehensive motifs. Another instance is what Blake calls in *Jerusalem*'s prose introduction a variation "both of cadences and number of syllables": "Every word and every letter is studied and put into its fit place: the terrific numbers are reserved for the terrific parts—the mild & gentle, for the mild & gentle parts, and the prosaic, for inferior parts: all are necessary to each other" (3, E144). As this metrical format is carried out, the "parts" become complexes of poetic sound. Blake uses them as pitches of voice, called up irregularly on a moment-to-moment basis, and he does not gradually modulate from one to another as he would if he were subordinating them to the demands of linear narrative and thus creating tonal sections rather than interwoven tonal motifs. He achieves a dynamics much like that of music, and throughout his long-line verse transitions as sharp as the following in *The Four Zoas* are not uncommon:

> Jerusalem in slumbers soft lulld into silent rest
> Terrific ragd the Eternal Wheels of intellect terrific ragd
> The living creatures of the wheels in the Wars of Eternal
>   life.   [I: 20: 11–13, E309]

Blake is not shifting into a new sequence, but this transition occurs three lines before the end of the book.[22]

In his attempt to reconstitute poetry as an auditory medium, then, Blake evolves from a treatment of lyric as song or ballad, as words to be spoken or to be sung to a musical setting, to a treatment of epic as an auditory mode, not in the setting it suggests for itself but in the fundamental principles of its style. Behind his stylistic inclinations is a strong sense that utterances are perceived differently by eye and ear, that these differences are crucial to the kinds of total impact a poem can have, and, further, that poetry not only in its historical origins but still, perhaps, in its prereflective appeal to us is an oral mode and must be recovered as such for its lost powers to be activated. Consequently, his long poems ask to be inwardly perceived as speech and to be followed as conversations are followed.

But this description needs to be qualified in an important way. Blake chose to be a writer, rather than a troubadour or a preacher, and his poetry was meant to be read. What we find in his poetic manner is an extraordinarily successful attempt to remake the written language into a medium of the speaking voice. Working within the visual medium of the page, he seeks an interplay between the perspectival expectations evoked by that medium and the auditory structure of the utterance itself, just as in his graphic work he seeks the effects of medieval manuscript illumination within the Renaissance medium of the engraved plate. A strife of sensory contraries is therefore built into Blake's verse at a primal level, for the reader, merely through the act of reading, is invited to participate in the warfare of eye and ear.[23] (The reader who resists the invitation will find it difficult to feel comfortable with Blake.) Two conclusions can be drawn from this. The first is that Blake is ultimately not interested in creating a mode purely of the ear, but rather in using the ear to oppose the tyranny of sight, with the goal of drawing the eye into an energetic interplay of equals. The second is that Blake's style serves directly the large purposes of his vision, for it is itself an instrument of sensory alteration and gives us one example of what he means by a cleansing of the doors of perception.

Smell, Vision, and Touch

I have suggested in the discussion of the ear that poetic speaking is so intimately related to a new order of visual appearances that it goes beyond the sense of hearing into synesthesia—seeing with ear and voice—and that auditory emphasis is not an end in itself but a means to a reorganized relationship among the senses. How, exactly, are the senses other than hearing affected in this reorganization?

The outlines of sensory transformation are most clearly discerned in the case of smell. The olfactory sense tends to be invoked in literary description with two sorts of special implication. As the dominant perceptual organ of animals, it opens the path for a writer such as Norman Mailer to portray a human embodiment at once vitalistic and magically unified with all natural existence. In its second role the sense of smell, with its haunting and far-reaching powers of evocation, offers a connection between the body of the present and the body of the past, as in Proust.[24] The latter project, a Wordsworthian one, would have no appeal for Blake, who regarded memory as the destroyer of inspiration. The sense of smell appears in his imagery chiefly in its symbolic connections with sexuality, but his usage is distinguished from Mailer's in that the odors of Luvah do not take us back to our animal origins but instead prefigure a breakthrough to the anti-natural humanity of Eden. In the following image, a liberation of sexual beauty is suggested as the vegetated energy, sharply repellent and poisonous to senses closed by moral virtue, is plucked and now seems newly sweet:

> The Wild Thyme is Los's Messenger to Eden, a mighty
> Demon

Terrible deadly & poisonous his presence in Ulro dark
Therefore he appears only a small Root creeping in grass
Covering over the Rock of Odours his bright purple mantle
Beside the Fount above the Larks nest in Golgonooza
Luvah slept here in death & here is Luvahs empty Tomb
Ololon sat beside this Fountain on the Rock of Odours.

[M. II: 35: 54–60, E135]

The intimation is that the loss of virginity denaturalizes the body, uproots it from the earth of Generation. The flight of the Wild Thyme, or the transport of odor, is the resurrection of Luvah, and it takes us not to the lower level of Beulah, or childhood, but to the upper, the higher innocence of sexual pleasure. Clearing a way through the veil of Vala and the closed sky of Urizen, it serves as a harbinger of the Edenic renewal.

Similarly, in the apocalyptic vintage at the end of *The Four Zoas,* the monster of sexual energy—here, a bull, Luvah's appearance among the animals, and one with particular sexual resonances in mythological tradition—now appears gentle: "And he shall lick the little girls white neck & on her head / Scatter the perfume of his breath" (IX: 135: 16–17, E388).

The natural body is harvested through perceptual abundance, a sudden joy in the things of the senses released by a deep forgiveness of sexual energy. From the winepresses of Luvah arise the "plentiful Odors of life," singing the delights of the body's resurrection. One is reminded of Blake's image of the flower's expansive fragrance, which has its source in "so small a center." In the same way, so small a center as the natural body is the source of the titanic exuberance Blake expresses in Luvah's vintage. It should be noted that Luvah's renewal, with its wines and aromas, comprehends the sense of taste, which has no consistent place either among Blake's eternal faculties or among his fallen organs. Luvah's power returns from the eye to an original faculty of savoring, in which lost possibilities of pleasure are regained; in the body's final reintegration in *Jerusalem,* the "Nerves of the Expansive Nostrils" are located "East in Rivers of bliss" (IV: 98: 16–17, E255). One theme of sensory improvement is thus a restoration of the unique and original function of a faculty, as if Blake were saying that our particular senses are trying at present to fill roles for which they are not equipped. This would include Los's sense of hearing when in the Urizenic portion of his career he uses it as a second-rate eye with which to copy nature.

The nostrils are also involved in the recurrent imagery of respiration. Blake tells us that the nostrils, closed in flesh and turned to the ground, have lost contact with the atmosphere of Eden, the Divine Breath or the wind of inspiration. There, breathing is afflatus, but our fallen respiratory sustenance is the air of the void, the invisible filling of our pure space. When the Divine Breath breathes over the morning hills at Albion's awakening, it is depicted as something felt over the whole body. The breath of Eternal Life seems to strike man tactually, and breathing becomes an embrace. Thus, as the nostrils in their olfactory aspect verge upon the senses of taste and, also, touch, in the sexuality of the great vintage, here again in their respiratory aspect they begin to lose a compartmentalized character and comprehend effects associated with other natural organs. The second theme of renewal is that each sense gains in richness and power as it is brought into relationship with others; the closer Blake gets in his imagery to the description of Eden, the more difficult it is to distinguish clearly between the five senses, precisely because the five-sense bodily system is breaking down.

The same dual process of a restoration to an original function and a renewed relationship to the other senses is evident in the improvement of sight. Earlier we noted the

imagery of the eyes that pervades the description of Tharmas'
separation from Enion. When, at the close of *The Four
Zoas*, the two are reunited as children in Beulah, their renewal is also portrayed in terms of the eyes. Presiding over
their union is Vala, for the emanation of man's emotional
faculty now teaches the innocence of sexuality and encourages us to modulate the distances of the eye with the
intimacies of the sense of touch:

> O my sweet Children Enion let Tharmas kiss thy Cheek
> Why dost thou turn thyself away from his sweet watry eyes
> Tharmas henceforth in Valas bosom thou shalt find sweet
> peace
> O bless the lovely eyes of Tharmas & the Eyes of Enion
>
> . . . . .
>
> Why weepest thou Tharmas Child of tears in the bright
> house of joy
> Doth Enion avoid the sight of thy blue heavenly Eyes
> And dost thou wander with my lambs & wet their innocent
> faces
> With thy bright tears because the steps of Enion are in the
> gardens
> Arise sweet boy & let us follow the path of Enion.
>
> [IX: 130: 22–31, E384]

The implications of this passage are radical, since the eye
is being redeemed specifically in its sexual phase; and Blake
is arguing, as he does elsewhere, against the darkness and
secrecy in which we characteristically seclude our love, as if
hiding it from our own accusing eyes:

> Are not the joys of morning sweeter
> Than the joys of night
> And are the vigrous joys of youth
> Ashamed of the light
>
> Let age & sickness silent rob
> The vineyards in the night

But those who burn with vigrous youth
Pluck fruits before the light.   [E463]

The new eyes of Enion and Tharmas are always of love,
never of accusation. These are the eyes of Upper Beulah,
which identify another as distinct, but beloved in its
distinction.[25]

The particular importance of such passages is their insistence that it is not the eye in itself that Blake resists, but the
perspectival eye, and it is this distinction that separates him
irrevocably from any program of transcending sight by simply refusing the visual. Blake maintains that we have many
eyes and that perspectivism is only one potentiality of vision.
In the natural world, we are capable of three distinct modes
of sight: the generative vision of differentiation and distance;
the Ulro vision of willful blindness, self-absorption, or accusation; and the Beulah vision of intimacy and fluidity, in
which visuality is modified by sensation of another order,
such as erotic touch or evocative smell. Edenic vision is a
way of seeing that is wholly beyond perspective; here, seeing
becomes a total knowledge, and there is no longer any dis-
parity between the visible and the demands of feeling and
imagination.[26]

That such vision is a possibility of the organ we now
have and is foreshadowed in the visual freedom available to
the artist is the theme of Blake's writings on painting, which
he regarded as a project to renovate sight. Just as he objects
to the Augustan couplet as a pre-existent container and a
mill which grinds out homogeneous grains, and to associa-
tionist psychological theory which hypothesizes the development of complex ideas, or generalities, out of homogeneous
atoms of sensation, so Blake objects to any style of painting
which emphasizes color and light over form, using them to
produce one "generalizing tone": "Such Harmony of Colour-
ing is destructive of Art One Species of General Hue over
all is the Cursed Thing calld Harmony it is like the Smile of

a Fool" (Ann. to Reynolds, E651). For Blake identity resides
in individual form, and the submergence of form in color
can only give us pictures of the void: "These are the Idiots
chiefest arts / To blend & not define the Parts" (E505). The
integrity of the whole depends on the integrity of each of its
individual parts: "All Genius varies(.) Thus Devils are various Angels are all alike" (E667). Indeed, things exist to the
extent that they have sharply discriminated forms:

If losing and obliterating the outline constitutes a Picture, Mr. B.
will never be so foolish as to do one. Such art of losing the outlines is the art of Venice and Flanders; it loses all character, and
leaves what some people call, expression: but this is a false notion of expression; expression cannot exist without character as
its stamina; and neither character nor expression can exist without firm and determinate outline. . . . The great and golden
rule of art, as well as of life, is this: That the more distinct,
sharp, and wirey the bounding line, the more perfect the work of
art. . . . How do we distinguish the oak from the beech, the
horse from the ox, but by the bounding outline? How do we
distinguish one face or countenance from another, but by the
bounding line and its infinite inflexions and movements? . . .
Leave out this l(i)ne and you leave out life itself; all is chaos
again, and the line of the almighty must be drawn out upon it
before man or beast can exist.   [D.C., E540]

Blake goes still further: "The Infinite alone resides in
Definite & Determinate Identity" (J. III: 55, E203). It is
with this conception of outline that Blake very clearly breaks
with the Sublime, which, in its rebellion against pictorialism,
sought the spacious in the deliberately vague, the infinite in
the boundless. Like the "Sensibility" poet of the early "Mad
Song," the Sublime found in Pope's feared Universal Darkness a way out of the vaulted day of Enlightenment; Blake
learned from the Sublime, but his Eden, with its fiery illumination, is on the far side of that night.

Outline, in Blake's theory, is considerably more than an

outer visual border, but runs through every part of the
visionary percept. It is a line which must define a form in
all its minute particulars:

> so he who wishes to see a Vision; a perfect Whole
> Must see it in its Minute Particulars; Organized & not as
>   thou
> O Fiend of Righteousness pretendest; thine is a Disorganized
> And snowy cloud: brooder of tempests & destructive War.

For "General Forms have their vitality in Particulars: &
every / Particular is a Man; a Divine Member of the Divine
Jesus" (J. IV: 91: 20–30, E249). The General Good is a single
law for the ox and the lion, and the Spectre of Albion, the
"Destroyer of Definite Form," builds deserts out of sand
grains; but, "All Sublimity is founded on Minute Discrimination" (Ann. to Reynolds; E632): "Labour well the Minute
Particulars, attend to the Little-ones" (J. III: 55: 51, E203).
The visibility of the given object is enlarged through our
attention to the precise minutiae that express its distinct
form, and to such an expansion of sight and of the object
there is no set limit.

In that Blake's contour is to be perceived in every part of
the form, and not simply in its border, it is a line resembling
that described by Da Vinci: "The secret of the art of drawing
is to discover in each object the particular way in which a
certain flexous line, which is, so to speak, its generating axis,
is directed through its whole extent" [27]—except that for
Blake, the metaphor of a generating axis is a step in the
direction of making the line a visible, pre-existent entity.
Blake's outline is an achievement, rather than a starting
point: "The Venetian and Flemish practice is broken lines,
broken masses, and broken colours. Mr. B.'s practice is unbroken lines, unbroken masses, and unbroken colours. Their
art is to lose form, his art is to find form, and to keep it"
(D.C., E529).

The fallen parody of the outline is the horizon or containing boundary, a Covering Cherub to prohibit the particularity of expansion. When line is conceived as something, in Merleau-Ponty's words, "outside living beings," it is externalized as an absolute and becomes an unrestrained Devourer, consuming imagination, digesting it into an aggregate of visual percepts with identical structures. Referring to Klee and Matisse, Merleau-Ponty speaks of a contrary "musing line," which does not circumscribe, but is rather the means by which a form comes into its own being: "Making its way in space, it nevertheless corrodes prosaic space." [28] This description can be applied to Blake's concept of line, for the boundaries of Urizen are corroded by a line that expresses individual choice. Like the fallen sense, the redeemed eye has the function of defining limits, but the difference is that while the natural eye imposes *a priori* bounds, redeemed vision seeks out the contours of fulfillment. The new outlines are the "lineaments of gratified desire," and the gratification subsists in the achievement of a specificity of form and act; beyond the outline of identity both ways is a globe of despair. Since form in Blake is the realization of desire, its contours cannot be set, but must constantly change with desire. Fire is the elemental image of such a form; and the contours of fire are perceived not in single bounding lines but throughout: it is the form which is all line. Geoffrey Hartman writes of an analogous flexibility of line in Rilke, in whose imagery he discerns a search for objects in which "a physical force has sought a certain kind of weight and balance at which the contour of visible things is not conceived as static and predetermined, but at the mercy of some perpetual inner fountain which, although achieving momentary balance, continually endangers the object's contour and enclosed nature, liable at any moment to burst forth." [29]

Blake's description of what the redeemed eye sees goes further than "the lineaments of gratified desire," and he is

quite clear about what the ultimate contours are. He con-
trasts to the "swelld & bloated General Forms" of Satan,

> the Divine-
> Humanity, who is the Only General and Universal Form
> To which all Lineaments tend & seek with love & sympathy
> All broad & general principles belong to benevolence
> Who protects minute particulars, every one in their own
> identity.   [J. II: 38: 19–23, E183]

The outlines of the Edenic percept are those of a man. In
the moment of fully imaginative perception, all things live
as men, or as one man, to whom one speaks as a friend, and
this is the final vision of *Jerusalem*. When Blake writes that
Tree Metal Earth & Stone are *identified* as human, the concepts of identification and identity refer, as they always do in
his work, not to a mental act but to a visual outline.

The percept of the redeemed eye, in its contours, has a
tactile character; and, in the quickness of its transformations,
it resembles the aural percept, for the ear, unlike the eye, is
oriented to fluid and continuous temporal changes. The visionary eye is strongly synesthetic, but it is still the eye and
not another sense: "These blots of light and dark, as being
the result of labour, are always clumsy and indefinite; the
effect of rubbing out and putting in, like the progress of a
blind man, or of one in the dark, who feels his way, but does
not see it" (E671). The visionary eye is the eye no longer externalized and drastically separated from the other senses,
but now reintegrated into Albion's fourfold body; and in its
regathering from a tyrannical position, it becomes a stronger,
rather than weaker, organ.

The sense of touch brings us to the limits of sensory improvement within the natural world. In that it represents
the complete body as a functioning unit, it has fallen farthest
from Eden, as the ear has fallen least; Albion cannot simply

rise from his rock and walk into paradise, but he has first to be awakened through his sense of hearing: "And in the Nerves of the Ear, (for the Nerves of the Tongue are closed) / On Albions Rock Los stands creating the glorious Sun each morning" (M. I: 29: 40–41, E126). Once the cosmic man has been aroused, however, the faculty of actualization is described as a tactile, rather than auditory, one.

The sense of touch seems sometimes to include taste [30] and, indeed, is particularly identified with the tongue, in both its tactile and its lingual functions: "the little tongue consum'd, that once in thoughtless joy / Gave songs of gratitude to waving corn fields round their nest" (F.Z., I, 17: 6–7, E306). The association of touch and tongue is so close in Blake's usage that it would perhaps be more accurate to call the faculty "tongue," reserving the word "touch" for its activity. The comprehensiveness of the organ forces itself on our attention as we track down the imagery of the other senses. As we have seen, it merges, most importantly, with the sense of hearing in the act of speech; and the improvements of smell or savoring, in the form of sexual pleasure, and of sight, in the form of outline, take these senses, as well, into the domain of the tactile. Touch summarizes all the sensory modes that are suppressed by the perspectival eye; and it is also the unifying faculty of the redeemed senses, the one through which they, quite literally, come in contact with each other. Because of its radical position, it is the source of mobility and the power to act, the capacity of execution without which imagination can never live. It also suggests the intimacy and the proximity that characterize renewed perception. The new senses discover space, for instance, not as what Lawrence called "a dreary on and on," [31] but as an intimate home, which is at the same time infinitely expansive because it can be moved at will by the perceiver:

> The Sky is an immortal Tent built by the Sons of Los
> And every Space that a Man views around his dwelling-place:

Standing on his own roof, or in his garden on a mount
Of twenty-five cubits in height, such space is his Universe;
And on its verge the Sun rises & sets. the Clouds bow
To meet the flat Earth & the Sea in such an orderd Space:
The Starry heavens reach no further but here bend and set
On all sides & the two Poles turn on their valves of gold:
And if he move his dwelling-place, his heavens also move.

[M. I: 29: 4–12, E126]

Both Keats and Lawrence present touch as the unifying sense of a liberated perception as clearly as does Blake. "Bright Star," with its image of lovers in a perpetual rhythmic repose, is perhaps the most striking manifestation of Keats's urge toward heaviness, palpability, and a durable shared vitality.[32] Lawrence writes of Etruscan painting:

They really have the sense of touch; the people and the creatures are all really in touch. It is one of the rarest qualities, in life as well as in art. There is plenty of pawing and laying hold, but no real touch. In pictures especially, the people may be in contact, embracing or laying hands on one another. But there is no soft flow of touch. The touch does not come from the middle of the human being. It is merely a contact of surfaces, and a juxtaposition of objects. This is what makes so many of the great masters boring, in spite of all their clever composition. Here, in this faded Etruscan painting, there is a quiet flow of touch that unites the man and the woman on the couch, the timid boy behind, the dog that lifts his nose, even the very garlands that hang from the wall.[33]

In both writers, as in Blake, a sense of deep and limitless communion with the other and with the total environment is felt through a heightened faculty of touch (although, again, for Blake touch has wider connotations).

In nature, little remains of the original faculty; indeed, its great power of love and action is largely twisted into hostility and impotence: "But here the affectionate touch of the tongue is closd in by deadly teeth" (J. II: 38: 24, E183).

Man's matter, his instincts, his bodily processes, his sexual energy, were all once perceived as benevolent; but now the Tree of Life is guarded by

> Tharmas the Vegetated Tongue even the Devouring Tongue:
> A threefold region, a false brain: a false heart:
> And false bowels: altogether composing the False Tongue,
> Beneath Beulah: as a watry flame revolving every way.
>
> [J. I: 14: 4–7, E156]

As touch summarizes the renewed senses, its spectre summarizes the fallen body as a whole. The cognitive faculty is transformed into a consuming perspectival brain; the emotional becomes a jealous and aggressive natural heart, whose blood is itself the nourishment of the Daughters of Albion; and the naturalized instincts are organized in the mill-like process of the digestive cycle. What we take to be contact is really a devouring.

Further, when the self withdraws from its own substance, the body's capacity for action is diminished; its titanic energies are pushed away from us, and we lose the connection between desire and act. The loss is implicit in the sudden dissociation of Tharmas from an act of his body, a crisis that fallen man undergoes with varying degrees of intensity at every moment of his natural experience. In *The Book of Thel* Blake seems to be suggesting that the crisis assumes particular magnitude at the point of passage into adolescence, for the poem sharply distinguishes between a body of childhood and a mature body and offers the myth of a deep and disturbing option given to man at the time of transition. Thel, when she refuses the generative body because of her fears of death and sexuality and of the natural organization in which the senses seem at odds with each other, rejects the state of power represented by Generation and so assumes the utterly powerless body of Ulro, in which man no longer has any capacity at all for transforming his own environment. All of Blake's fallen characters (except Orc and the late Los) in one way or another refuse embodiment, even while they seek it; refused, the body becomes an instrument, then a cavern; and the ultimate fallen form of the tongue is the flaming sword of the Cherub. Here the liberty of the senses to discover and achieve their own fulfillment is replaced by a self-induced suppression and a feeling of powerlessness in the face of Nobodaddy's emissary angel—who is only the externalized and divided body of the perceiver: the body itself seems to stand in our way. Albion's volition is now as far from his capacity as his dreaming mind is from the rock on which he sleeps.

At the division of Tharmas, the immortals close the Gate of the Tongue in fear, and this Gate of Paradise remains locked until Los's work is finished. Blake always maintains a distinction between the power of conversing with Eden, which is at all times available to fallen man, and the power of actually entering it, which is not. The full reactivation of touch, however, takes us beyond a natural synesthesia possible in individual experience into a complete remaking of humanity; and it is thus to Blake's portrayals of the resurrection in *The Four Zoas* and *Jerusalem* that we must follow his imagery of the body.

CHAPTER 4

The Body of Imagination

The Risen Body

The belief in a resurrection of the body is a fundamental tenet in Swedenborg, and its articulation in his work, as well as in other mystical writings of Blake's experience, might well have stimulated Blake's own interest in the theme. Swedenborg describes the risen, or "angelic," body chiefly as a magnification of the natural organism. The senses are retained in their present structure, but they are sharpened: when outer sight is brought into alignment with spiritual sight, seeing becomes understanding, and the light of heaven enables angelic vision to distinguish the minutiae on which the perception of the Divine Humanity depends.[1] Occasionally, Swedenborg indicates, ambiguously, that "an angel has every sense that a man has, and far more exquisite senses."[2] But in these matters he never goes beyond assertion. Where he is descriptive, he deals with the perfection of the five senses, and, although he integrates them to the extent that each becomes a faculty for perceiving a certain aspect of the unific Divine Humanity (for example, the eye corresponds to wisdom, the ear to obedience), ultimately he keeps them independent of one another. And sometimes he splits them in valuations which in Blake would amount to another fall:

But the rest of the senses with the angels are less exquisite than
the senses of seeing and hearing, for the reason that seeing and
hearing serve their intelligence and wisdom, and the rest do not;
and if the other senses were equally exquisite they would detract
from the light and joy of their wisdom, and would let in the delight of pleasures pertaining to various appetites and to the body;
and so far as these prevail they obscure and weaken the understanding. This is seen in the world, where men become gross and
stupid in regard to spiritual truths so far as they indulge in the
sense of taste and yield to the allurements of the sense of touch.[3]

What resemblances there are to Blake are very general,
and the treatment of the angelic body does not help us a
great deal with the intricacies of Blake's verse; it is best regarded as source material, which the poet's imagination ran-
sacked for what it could use. Blake's most direct influences in
the portrayal of a risen body are Ezekiel, Isaiah, St. John of
Patmos, and Milton; and the closest parallels in our own
century are to be found in Rilke and Lawrence. But the most
immediate context of the Blakean resurrection is the titanism
of his age, the revolutionary enthusiasm that, in the last
pages of the *Enquiry Concerning Political Justice,* drove
Godwin to the edges of the Enlightenment when he suggested that man could evolve a human body such as he had
never known, one liberated from disease and suited to the
power and the freedom of an unshackled consciousness, one
able for the first time to truly live. The myth of a new body,
possible here and now, haunts the imagery of Wordsworth,
Coleridge, Shelley, and Keats; and, outside Blake, it receives
its most explicit elaboration in *Prometheus Unbound,* with
its description of the transfiguration of Asia, the reintegration of both the sole self and the formerly inanimate into a
joyous and personal universal body, and the regeneration of
substance into radiance, music, dance, and the "perpetual
Orphic song" of renovated communication.

In Night IX of *The Four Zoas,* Blake describes the resurrection of Albion through the successive renewals of each of his members and their reintegration into a community of creative work. The final movement of the apocalypse begins with Urizen's confession of ultimate failure:

> Seeking the Eternal which is always present to the wise
> Seeking for pleasure which unsought falls round the infants
>   path
> And on the fleeces of mild flocks who neither care nor
>   labour.   [121: 10–12, E375]

Albion by this time has been redeemed to the point of re-calling his members, and the first to be regathered is the Prince of Light. It is strange at first glance that Urizen is the hero of the last book; but in the terms of Blake's myth this irony has compelling justification. The action of Night IX pivots on Urizen's surrender of self-consciousness and of his Faustian quest to carve out futurity with an imperial reason and will, and its theme is the reintegration of consciousness into the complete body of man. Thus, in a reversal that is as striking conceptually as it is dramatically, a redeemed No-bodaddy takes the lead in the work of renovation. He recognizes now that the world of nature is not an end in itself but a seedbed, and, in the sustained figure of the apoc-alyptic harvest that dominates the book, it is he who sows the human seed and reaps the "wide Universe."

In the joyful work of creating a new human condition and in the sensuous richness of the Dionysiac banquet with which the first phase of the apocalypse culminates, the beginnings of a reintegrated and enlarged human experience are mani-fest. At the same time, this "rural work" is felt among men as the revolutionary "pangs of Eternal Birth," and as the labors progress the spectres are consumed in the fires of Urizen's renovated consciousness, to re-emerge in new bodies. The emanations return to the Zoas, and the Zoas to their proper places. Luvah and Vala leave the brain and heart and

return to the loins, and as Luvah gathers back his emanation
the Golden Age begins anew: "Come forth O Vala from the
grass & from the silent Dew / Rise from the dews of death
for the Eternal Man is Risen" (126: 31–32, E380). Tharmas
and Enion are renewed as children of a reorganized Innocence:

> And when Morning began to dawn upon the distant hills
> a whirlwind rose up in the Center & in the Whirlwind a
>   shriek
> And in the Shriek a rattling of bones & in the rattling of
>   bones
> A dolorous groan & from the dolorous groan in tears
> Rose Enion like a gentle light.   [132: 13–17, E385]

As the Zoas return, the possibilities of the human body
gradually expand. At the harvest feast in Urizen's once desolate South, they celebrate their reunion and, embracing the
"New Born Man," commit themselves to a new faith:

> Not for ourselves but for the Eternal family we live
> Man liveth not by Self alone but in his brothers face
> Each shall behold the Eternal Father & love & joy abound.
>   [133: 24–26, E387]

The parts of Albion's body no longer work against each other
but are now "Cooperating in the bliss of Man obeying his
Will" (126: 16, E380).

   Thus far the Zoas have risen to the State of Upper Beulah,
where they are first refreshed on couches of "sweet repose"
and then rise to enjoy the furious revels of Luvah's vintage,
which are experienced among men both as a sudden release
of pleasure and as the agonies of revolutionary change. The
intoxications of Beulah are such, however, that for a moment
it seems as if the renovation is to be drowned in its newly
discovered fulfillments. As the revels develop, they turn
destructive: the children of Luvah "catch the Shrieks in cups
of gold they hand them to one another / These are the sports

of love & these the sweet delights of amorous play" (137: 1–2, E390).

It is clear that man is not yet ready for a final celebration. The festival, when taken as an end in itself, is a false dawn, in which the apocalypse is in danger of being deflected back into the world of Tirzah. But at this juncture Albion urges the Zoas to further labor, and they work together in a second harvest, this one of grain. Since the triumph of Luvah needs to be regarded as a beginning of the rise from Beulah to Eden, he is "put for dung on the ground" (24); the corn is stored by Urizen and sifted by Tharmas; and the fourth Zoa, the maker Urthona, rises in "all his regenerate power" to bake the "Bread of Ages." The bread and wine of a new human substance are now prepared, even as the world beneath reaches its wintry nadir of sorrow. The new joys force the contrast between oppression and liberation to a breaking point, and a new universe at last bursts forth:

> The Sun has left his blackness & has found a fresher morning
> And the mild noon rejoices in the clear & cloudless night
> And Man walks forth from midst of the fires the evil is all consumd
> His eyes behold the Angelic spheres arising night & day
> The stars consumd like a lamp blown out & in their stead behold
> The Expanding Eyes of Man behold the depths of wondrous worlds
>
> One Earth one sea beneath nor Erring Globes wander but Stars
> Of fire rise up nightly from the Ocean & one Sun
> Each morning like a New born Man issues with songs & Joy
> Calling the Plowman to his Labour & the Shepherd to his rest
> He walks upon the Eternal Mountains raising his heavenly voice
> Conversing with the Animal forms of wisdom night & day

That risen from the Sea of fire renewd walk oer the Earth.

[138: 20–32, E391]

Man's marvelous powers of speech and vision indicate that he is qualitatively beyond the joyful body of Beulah. But Blake suggests that even this is only a beginning. The poem closes with a triumphant Urthona preparing the arms of intellect, which, now that war and the "dark Religions" have departed, will take man into the day of a full and human consciousness, one that Blake calls a "sweet Science." Blake is here not so much at odds with the Enlightenment as surpassing it in comprehensiveness. Night IX shows us an expansion of consciousness beyond the limits of the self and of orthodox rationality, its commitment to the discovery and the building of a new age for all men, and the restoration of its connections with loins, emotions, what we would call the unconscious (Blake's animal world, his water world of Tharmas, and his Beulah dream world) and the body as a whole. The development is one from reason to "intellect," or imagination, from a dark science of abstractionism and a "Stern Philosophy" of good and evil [4] to the sweet science of the last line.

The resurrection in *The Four Zoas* is thus based on a reorganization of action, rather than a final repose from it; on the renascence of an integrated sensibility beyond self-consciousness; and on a far-reaching myth of brotherhood that includes a brotherhood of the faculties and senses. The closing plates of *Jerusalem* reaffirm these motifs but go far beyond them. In the new treatment, the apocalypse is at once more embattled in its accomplishment and more radical in its propositions. The pervasiveness and the recalcitrance of the natural self appear substantially greater, and the sense of struggle and affliction is more immediate because it is attributed not to the "human grapes," or society at large, but directly to the central characters, Albion and his Zoas. Thus the renewal is given the narrative structure not of a

harvest but of a battle against the embodiment of the Satanic
selfhood, the Covering Cherub; and the dynamics of brotherhood are extended in the themes of self-sacrifice and forgiveness, on which a human resurrection now pivots. Los-Jesus
is now the sole agent of regeneration, for Blake seems convinced that no mode of consciousness other than artistic can
free itself sufficiently from the restrictions of the spectre to
experience a Divine Vision.[5]

When Albion awakes, he compels the Zoas to return to
their original places of work: Tharmas to the sheepfold,
Urizen to the plow, and Luvah to the Loom; Urthona is
already at his anvil in the form of the "Great Spectre Los."
However, once Albion arises from the fires of self-sacrifice,
we see the Zoas no longer in a community but in a fourfold
oneness. When the Eternal Man reaches for his bow, the
Zoas reach for their own bows; but there is a single "horned
Bow Fourfold." In his description of the risen man Blake
emphasizes the unison of the body's functioning and the
actual process of the cooperation:

> And every Man stood Fourfold. each Four Faces had. One to
> the West
> One toward the East One to the South One to the North.
> the Horses Fourfold
> And the dim Chaos brightened beneath, above, around! Eyed
> as the Peacock
> According to the Human Nerves of Sensation, the Four
> Rivers of the Water of Life.   [IV: 98: 12–15, E254]

The senses, as we conceive them, drop out to be replaced by
faculties, which, as separate entities, themselves drop out to
be replaced by a fourfold organ of imagination, the body of
Albion. In their renewed unity the faculties are imaged as
Albion's bow, his chariots, the Four Rivers of Paradise, and
the circumference of Paradise, comprehending at once, then,
his activity, his life processes, and his bodily form.

The five natural organs of perception, functioning in separation, are one-dimensional contractions of the four-dimensional risen body. This much is clear from Blake's doctrinal statements, but what begins to become clear only in the imagery of these closing plates is the problem of "numerous senses." The Four Eternal Senses are Four Faces, each commanding a cardinal point, and yet each fourfold in itself. Albion can thus see in all directions at the same time. He has no set physical position *vis-à-vis* an object and is not limited to the directional fragmentation of natural vision. Similarly, there is no longer a distinction between center and circumference, because his faculties define the changing outline of his perceptual field. In accordance with this infinite flexibility of vision, the four faculties are described as "Eyed as the Peacock." The risen man has innumerable eyes, which collectively compose his faculty of vision. There is, then, no contradiction or ambiguity when Blake refers sometimes to four paradisaical faculties and sometimes to numerous or multiplied eternal senses. In Eden man has both infinite eyes and four senses.

The imagery of Albion's new body is dynamic to the extent that it is more accurate to describe it as a risen activity than as a risen body. Its fourfoldness is difficult, deliberately, to imagine in static, naturalistic terms; but it appears instead in the constant activity of the bow and arrow, the expansion and contraction of the faculties, and the chariots always "going forward forward irresistible from Eternity to Eternity" (98: 27, E255). A body, as we tend to think of it, is a set, basically pictorial form; but the body Blake describes subsists in its activity and its motion. The only actual visual image of the risen body Blake gives us, the four fourfold chariots in motion, is one which defies the powers of the natural eye. Like the chariot of Ezekiel, on which Blake bases it, it is unconditioned and self-impelled and moves through no spatiality external to itself:

> Whithersoever the spirit was to go, they went,
> thither *was their* spirit to go; and the wheels
> were lifted up over against them: for the spirit
> of the living creatures *was* in the wheels.   [1 : 20]

The following passage offers Blake's fullest portrayal of the
renovated body:

> And they conversed together in Visionary forms dramatic
>   which bright
> Redounded from their Tongues in thunderous majesty, in
>   Visions
> In new Expanses, creating exemplars of Memory and of
>   Intellect
> Creating Space, Creating Time according to the wonders
>   Divine
> Of Human Imagination, throughout all the Three Regions
>   immense
> Of Childhood, Manhood & Old Age(;) & the all tremendous
>   unfathomable Non Ens
> Of Death was seen in regenerations terrific or complacent
>   varying
> According to the subject of discourse & every Word & Every
>   Character
> Was Human according to the Expansion or Contraction, the
>   Translucence or
> Opakeness of Nervous fibres such was the variation of Time
>   & Space
> Which vary according as the Organs of Perception vary &
>   they walked
> To & fro in Eternity as One Man reflecting each in each &
>   clearly seen
> And seeing: according to fitness & order.   [28–40]

There is no distinction here between perception and creation, activity and receptivity, imagination and sensation. The
body has become the soul; the senses have been improved
until they can perceive everything that the Poetical Genius

can imagine; and the form of the risen body is like the form of fire in its continuous changes of contour, according to changes in impulse and desire.

Through the passage, images of voice, vision, sound, light, discourse, and creative power develop a radically synesthetic effect. As Ernest Tuveson has noted, "Abstraction is only one sense impression isolated from the others"; [6] and the risen body reveals the antithetical condition, more than an extraordinary modification of one sense by another, but a complete and normative interplay. Merleau-Ponty writes that perception is prereflectively a total sensory response, not a sum of visual, tactile, and audible givens,[7] but in Blake the final actualization of the synesthetic character of perception is a metamorphosis, giving us a body far different from the one we know. At this point, however, the concept of synesthesia requires some exact definition. What Blake implies is not a fusion of the faculties into one undifferentiated organic sense. The effect of synesthesia here, just as, for example, in Coleridge's "sound-like power in light" ("The Eolian Harp," 28) and Shelley's music "felt like an odour within the sense" ("The Sensitive Plant," I: 28), is not to erase distinctions between kinds of sensation but to play them off against one another, setting up a rich and mutually heightening interaction. Blake's risen body is founded not on a return to nonindividuation but on the individuality of minute particulars, and its character, in all respects, is dialectical. Suggestive at this point is a dialectic of the senses that Wordsworth regards as Nature's means of opposing the despotism of the eye; Nature

> summons all the senses each
> To counteract the other, and themselves
> And makes them all, and the objects with which all
> Are conversant, subservient in their turn
> To the great ends of Liberty and Power.
>
> [*The Prelude,* XII: 135–39]

And the relationship among the flowers in "The Sensitive Plant" is also similar to the kind of multifold unification that Blake's faculties display:

> For each one was interpenetrated
> With the light and the odour its neighbours shed,
> Like young lovers whom youth and love make dear
> Wrapped and filled by their mutual atmosphere.   [I: 66–69] [8]

The format assumed by sensory interrelationship in Blake is illuminated by the following verse from Ezekiel's description of the chariot:

> And when they went, I heard the noise of their
> wings, like the noise of great waters, as the
> voice of the Almighty, the voice of speech, as the
> noise of an host.   (1 : 24)

The activity of Albion's fully awakened body is a kind of speech, presented as the mode of the Zoas' interplay; and in this Edenic conversation, the action of all the faculties at once, the tongue creates thundering, visionary forms. It is a speech like poetry, with the difference that it is poetry actualized and the universe is directly created by the tongue. In this new language the improvement of the body and the improvement of human communication converge, as they also do, in a smaller way, in the paradise imagined by Keats in "I Stood Tip-Toe," where the lovers are joined to one another through a new efficacy of speech:

> Young men, and maidens at each other gaz'd
> With hands held back, and motionless, amaz'd
> To see the brightness in each other's eyes;
> And so they stood, fill'd with a sweet surprise,
> Until their tongues were loos'd in poesy.
> Therefore no lover did of anguish die:
> But the soft numbers, in that moment spoken,
> Made silken ties, that never may be broken.   [231–38]

As the description of Blake's Eden develops, more and more of existence is reclaimed by the new arts of vocalization, and forms regain their humanity as they join in the ever-expanding conversation of the risen body. Albion, now perceived as Jehovah, speaks "terrific from his Holy Place" (which is co-extensive with the body and the universe), in visible words of the Mutual Covenant Divine, the mutual humanity of perceiver and percept. This covenant is conveyed

> On Chariots of gold & jewels with Living Creatures starry &
> flaming
> With every Colour, Lion, Tyger, Horse, Elephant, Eagle
> Dove, Fly, Worm,
> And the all wondrous Serpent clothed in gems & rich array
> Humanize
> In the Forgiveness of Sins according to the Covenant of
> Jehovah . . . [42–45] [9]

The new covenant, Albion's perceptible attitude toward his objects, is the forgiveness that allows all things to realize their human status, a divine accord that everything is holy, everything a man; it is, indeed, a call for lion and tiger to assume human form. In answer they vocalize their awareness of the sudden disappearance of their generative state:

> Where is the Covenant of Priam, the Moral Virtues of the
> Heathen
> Where is the Tree of Good & Evil that rooted beneath the
> cruel heel
> Of Albions Spectre the Patriarch Druid! where are all his
> Human Sacrifices
> For Sin in War & in the Druid Temples of the Accuser of
> Sin: beneath
> The Oak Groves of Albion that coverd the whole Earth
> beneath his Spectre
> Where are the Kingdoms of the World & all their glory that
> grew on Desolation

The Fruit of Albions Poverty Tree when the Triple Headed
   Gog-Magog Giant
Of Albion Taxed the Nations into Desolation & then gave
   the Spectrous Oath

Such is the Cry from all the Earth from the Living Creatures
   of the Earth
And from the great City of Golgonooza in the Shadowy
   Generation
And from the Thirty-two Nations of the Earth among the
   Living Creatures.   [46–56, E256]

At last, beyond the redemption of animals, the inanimate—
tree, metal, earth, and stone—is returned to humanity; and
the landscape is consumed as the lost vocal power of objects is
recovered. Now the speech of the risen body is answered as
the human forms cry out the name of their emanations,
which in their unison are called Jerusalem, as the risen
speakers are in their interplay Albion.

The reorganization of the body includes a transformation
of man's substance, as well as his faculties and their percepts.
Judging from Blake's normal usage of the four elements, we
might expect fire—the renovative medium of Orc and, in
the late work, of Los at his forge, as well as the most malev-
olent of the elements in the form of the Cherub's sword—
to be the prime material of Eden, and it does remain the redemptive substance until Plate 96. But when Albion himself,
sacrificing his natural selfhood to save Los, plunges into the
fires, then: "the Furnaces became / Fountains of Living
Waters flowing from the Humanity Divine" (36–37, E253).
In the description that follows of the re-entry of all life into
Eden, fire is at first the predominant material, particularly in
the flaming arrows of mental warfare. Yet when Blake describes the weapons of the Zoas—Urizen's "breathing Bow
of carved Gold," Luvah's "Silver Bow bright shining,"
Tharmas' "Bow of Brass pure flaming richly wrought," and
Urthona's "Bow of Iron terrible thundering" (97: 7–11)—the

sense is not of fire, but of a comprehensive fiery matter, including such properties as silvery brightness, breathing, and thundering, as well as the attributes of specific metals. The final annihilation of the Druid Spectre is surrounded with aerial images: breath, clouds, wind, the illumination of "dim Chaos." Next, water returns in the figure of the reintegrated Zoas as the "Four Rivers of the Water of Life"; and this materiality drops out, in turn, to be replaced by gems, "gold and jewels," the precious substances of the earth which adorn the humanized forms. And in the last plate, tree, metal, earth, and stone are gathered into Eden. All four elements enter paradise; and there is finally a sense in the passage as a whole, although Blake is not explicit about this, of not one predominant element in Eden, nor even of air, earth, and water assuming the characteristics of fire, but of a new fourfold substance made from the reintegration of air, earth, water, and fire.

Blake describes the fall as a division of the elements: the Zoas collapse toward a center, which is now surrounded by four abandoned spheres: to the South, Urizen's world of burning fire; to the East, Luvah's void; to the West, Tharmas' world of raging waters; to the North, Urthona's "solid Darkness / Unfathomable without end" (J. III: 59: 19–20, E206). The implication is that the four elements in which our existence appears to us are divided portions of ourself. In the closing passage of *Jerusalem* there is no sense of a materiality distinct from human substance: fire, earth, air, and water are humanized, and together they compose the Edenic matter of man, who in his new body is fiery and fountain-like at the same time. Thus, what Blake describes, far from a dematerialization of man, is a regathering of his complete substance.

A further theme in the passage is that everything in Eden is directly available to perception and is of such closeness that it is impossible to abstract inside and outside from Blake's lines. J. H. van den Berg provides an effective analogue to this apocalyptic illumination when he writes that the visibility of God "is the nearness between man and man. When God is with us, He does not appear as a transparent ghost in the realm of the dead. He stands, face to face with us as an acquaintance, a friend, a wife, a husband, or a child." [10] Everything now is human and can be conversed with. There are no levels or orders of being, and everything is opened and revealed: Chaos brightens, the "Non Ens / Of Death was seen in regenerations." There are no dark and remote places, no spots of unconsciousness, and all is translucent, as once only the world within the center was. The discovery of a total presence and manifestation is an important tradition in the literature of apocalypse. In Ezekiel, for instance, God promises, "Neither will I hide my face any more from them" (39:29). In Blake's literal treatment, matter becomes radiant, as it is in the new world of *Prometheus Unbound* and in the lost, original landscape of Wordsworth's "Intimations of Immortality." A characteristic Blakean touch is that the illumination is not actually a property of Eden, for this is not a world of established qualities. Instead, the relative translucency or opacity of substance is under the perceiver's control. He can see up to or through, as he wishes, so determining his own horizons.

In the same way, time and space now have their being in the impulses of the risen body. They are originally, Blake tells us, "Real Beings a Male & a Female Time is a Man Space is a Woman & her Masculine Portion is death" (V.L.J., E553), or Los, Enitharmon, and the Spectre of Urthona. In nature they assume dehumanized form: spectral time is the mere accumulation of seconds and spectral space, the aggregation of inches. In Ulro there is, properly, no space or time at all, but feelings of void and of unending repetition. Man is contained by a rigid destiny and a limitless, meaningless extension. Blake's irony is that this is the immortality of the eye, in which seconds and inches are extended indefinitely, and it applies to our common imaginings of both the static monotony of heaven and the endless torments of hell. Los works to personalize time and space, to base them not on the atomistic units of their abstraction from activity but in the human time of a pulsation of an artery and in the human space of a globule of blood. His efforts begin to bear fruit in Beulah with its "watery delusions" of unification; there, space becomes intimate and qualitative, and moments of dream, play, and sexual love are experienced as "timeless." They are timeless, however, in the sense that activity takes primacy over its duration; the perceiver is not aware of a time or a space that is abstracted from his senses, feelings, and actions. But the delights of Beulah are chiefly personal; they offer relaxation from the pressures of positive time and space without finally consuming them. In Eden, time and space are reintegrated in what Frye identifies as the fourth dimension,[11] and they are fully returned to man, who now creates them in the rhythmic expansions and contractions of his risen body. For Blake, eternity and infinity involve not an emancipation from, but a reorganization of the sense of space and time. They signify the liberty to invent space and time, in the way that art does, and so to be alive in an immediate present that is delineated by the perceiver's imagination.

The visionary conversation is thus the making of life, now analogous to the making of a work of art, and in these plates Blake describes the achievement of a particular Edenic moment, in which desire finds its form and in which the natural world is replaced by a world of emanation. In the poem's final line, the moment is consummated as the emanation is joyfully recognized: a poem is completed, a world is made, Albion rejoins his bride. But there is no finality in this accomplishment, for Blake's paradise is not the end-point of a linear development, but a state of perpetual creative activity. Eden itself moves, going from Eternity to Eternity, creation to creation. "The discovery itself," writes Merleau-Ponty, "calls forth still further quests. . . . For painters the world will always be yet to be painted." [12]

Art and Eden

A problem that arises in conjunction with Albion's final awakening is that, reading Blake, particularly the poetry and prose after *The Four Zoas,* one often gets the impression that Eden and the experience of art are synonymous, and this identification can find considerable support. Blake writes in the *Descriptive Catalogue,* "The artist is an inhabitant of that happy country," or Eden (E533), and *Jerusalem* can be read as the story of the making of a single work of art, in its fullest psychic and social contexts, at the end of which Los is regathered into paradise. In a remarkable passage, Blake asserts that the same dwelling is available to the artist's public: "If the Spectator could Enter into these Images in his Imagination approaching them on the Fiery Chariot of his Contemplative Thought if he could Enter into Noahs Rainbow or into his bosom or could make a friend & Companion of one of these Images of wonder which always intreats him to leave mortal things as he must know then would he arise from his Grave then would he meet the Lord in the Air & then he would be happy" (V.L.J., E550). And in an 1801 letter to Flaxman, Blake congratulates the sculptor on the completion of his "Great Work," as follows: "The Kingdoms of this World are now become the Kingdoms of God & his Christ, & we shall reign with him for ever & ever. The Reign of Literature & the Arts Commences" (Oct. 19, 1801, E686). Such statements could be construed to indicate an identification of Golgonooza and Jerusalem, the city of art and the city of Eden. Frye is explicit about this: "The totality of imaginative power, of which the matrix is art, is what we ordinarily call culture or civilization." [13] Golgonooza is the edifice of human culture, where all the things of life are remade into their fully human and social forms. When it is finished, "nature, its scaffolding, will be knocked away and man will live in it. Golgonooza will then be the city of God, the New Jerusalem which is the total form of all human culture and civilization." [14]

I would suggest, however, that in the discursive passages above Blake is emphasizing a milder vision of the apocalypse than is created by his poetic narratives and imagery. Blake uses the concept of imagination to refer both to the fallen faculty through which paradise is reconstituted and to the reality of Eden, and the relationship between the two is an intricate one. In this section, I wish to review the distinction in light of the final renovation Blake depicts at the end of *Jerusalem*.[15]

The integral body of Albion survives the fall in the shrunken and scattered organs of sense. It survives in full form not as an accepted actuality but as the Divine Vision, kept by the poet-prophet when all others have forsaken it. The vision of Eden is not, however, a peculiar possession of the artist, for imagination exists in all men as the original, universal, and highest phase of our human consciousness, and it makes itself felt in the natural texture of our lives as a divine intercessor: "What is the Divine Spirit? is the Holy Ghost any other than an Intellectual Fountain?" (J. III: 77, E229). The intellectual fountain does not belong to our natural inheritance but is the part of us that falls into the world in our natural birth, to be enclosed in a cavern-like body. Independent of nature, it can only be diminished by memory, experiential wisdom, or any mental process in which a blank space is filled with sensations, information, or ideas from without. Its inexhaustible energy cannot be acquired but is available to all men through inspiration; and inspiration to Blake is at once a generous opening of the mind and the senses and a labor of copying "(Imagination)

The Holy Ghost," rather than the "Goddess Nature (Memory)" (E668). "Genius and Inspiration are the great Origin and Bond of Society" (D.C., E518), for in their imaginations all men inhabit a home where everything is equally holy and human. Blake shares with Marx the conviction that community is not a development of man's history but an original mode of relationship, from which history has been a continuing fall into isolation. But this final home is for Blake available only through the uncompromised uniqueness of individual perception. Keats, in the letter to John Hamilton Reynolds of February 19, 1818, beautifully illuminates not only Blake but the way in which English Romanticism tries to see beyond the dualism of the community and the individual that still today conditions our thinking about perception and about politics: "But the Minds of Mortals are so different and bent on such diverse Journeys that it may at first appear impossible for any common taste and fellowship to exist between two or three under these suppositions—It is however quite the contrary—Minds would leave each other in contrary directions, traverse each other in Numberless points, and [at] last greet each other at the Journeys end." Blake would go even farther, for at the end of *The Four Zoas* and *Jerusalem* the individual discovers both a full sense of community and a full sense of particularity, neither of which can exist without the other.

The imagination, as opposed to the perspective of the mind's eye, is the true universalization; it is a unific, although infinitely various, world for all men, and thus a sphere of absolute truth: "All Forms are Perfect in the Poets Mind. but these are not Abstracted nor Compounded from Nature (but are from Imagination)" (Ann. to Reynolds, E637). In the *Laocoön*, Blake writes: "The Eternal Body of Man is The Imagination. that is God Himself The Divine Body. . . . It manifests itself in his Works of Art" (E271). And since all art potentially opens a path to the same universal home, Eden, there is ultimately no value hierarchy of artists or art-works: "To suppose that Art can go beyond the finest specimens of Art that are now in the world, is not knowing what Art is; it is being blind to the gifts of the spirit" (D.C., E535). Blake can carry this understanding of art to startling lengths; it would seem, for example, that in his inspired work, in vocalizing his vision of Eden, the poet necessarily speaks truth, as if "truth" were by definition the content of enthusiastic poetic song: "I am Inspired! I know it is Truth! / For I Sing" (M. I: 13: 51, E107).

Thus Blake says far more than that the imagination is one of our valid powers, with its own laws and its own species of knowledge. Imagination is, rather, our whole power, the total functioning interplay of our capacities. The work of the artist is to actualize this innate cooperation as an environment for all men. Since the fall consists in a division of paradise into the spiritual and bodily portions of Divine Vision and organs of perception, the restorative work consists in rebuilding the connections between the two, or expanding the latter to the fullness of the former. That art should be the agency of this rapprochement is not surprising, for it is quite orthodoxly conceived of as a mode of knowing that participates simultaneously in soul and body, a mental work of the senses and feelings. However, Blake finds in the very nature of art, with its distinctly sensuous and affective mode of consciousness, an apocalyptic potentiality.

But the healing possibilities of art are realized only when esthetic pleasure and cognition are conceived of as an acid bath for the natural world, rather than as its complement or decoration, and it is with this purpose that Los builds his great city. Golgonooza is originally constructed in an act of compassion, as a refuge for the imaginative forms which have been exiled from the worlds of single and double vision:

> The stones are pity, and the bricks, well wrought affections:
> Enameld with love & kindness, & the tiles engraven gold
> Labour of merciful hands: the beams & rafters are forgive-
>   ness.   [see J. I: 12: 30–37, E154]

Here, in the realm of fallen art, natural objects are transformed into poetic percepts. Golgonooza is the imaginative
version of the fallen city of man, a "Spiritual fourfold London," and within its scope things are seen in their relation to
man and walls are not slabs of stone but "faces." The building of the city, constantly assaulted by all that is not yet art, is
a labor akin to the writing of the one great poem to which,
says Shelley, all poets are contributors; and the force of art,
once it recognizes its own subversive nature, is incremental,
eventually assuming the proportions of a counter-creation.

  Golgonooza, as noted above, is founded on "London
Stone," depicted as the world-center, the omphalos, or nexus
with another mode of being. That fallen art, built in nature,
does annex us by a new kind of consciousness to something
more than the world of our natural perception and natural
reason, suggests that it is potentially the point of entry to a
new world. But Blake is quite explicit about what Golgonooza
does not contain: "Go on, builders in hope: tho Jerusalem
wanders far away, / Without the gate of Los: among the dark
Satanic wheels" (J. I: 12: 43–44, E154). And in describing the
fourfold directionality of the city, Blake writes: "But that
toward Eden is walled up, till time of renovation" (52). Both
Jerusalem and paradise are outside the dimension of the
fallen art form. We know of their existence through art, and,
Blake says, the more trust we place in the works of the poetic
imagination, the firmer our conviction of an Edenic possibility becomes. But Albion's final reunion with the departed
emanation and his actual re-entry into the paradisaical state
of human integration is not achieved within the limits of
fallen art. Fallen art, in Blake, always occupies an ambivalent
position, at once sharing the horizons of the fall and liberated

from them, both fundamentally opposed to all our limitations and finally subject to them.

The same passage corroborates the distinction in another way. Blake clearly locates Golgonooza within the world of suffering: "Around Golgonooza lies the land of death eternal; a Land / Of pain and misery and despair and ever brooding melancholy" (13: 30–31, E155). And he goes on to show us Cave, Rock, Tree, and all the terrors of Ulro "on all sides surrounding / Golgonooza." Roughly, Golgonooza is to Jerusalem as Spenser's Cleopolis is to his New Jerusalem. It contains the best of this world and it is a haven; but just as there is a fallen distinction between art and life, so Golgonooza is art within nature. The city Jerusalem, on the other hand, replaces the world of pain, and in Eden the distinction of art and life vanishes. Art, as we know it, is thus not an end but a way. It is able to take its impetus from the world of imagination, the Divine Vision sheltered within, and it is able to open up that world and bring us to the point of entering it; but, in itself, it remains less than Edenic. To suggest, as Hazard Adams and Karl Kiralis do, that the poem *Jerusalem* is written as an example of Divine Vision [16] is, obviously, to open the poem to the kind of attack no human artifact could possibly sustain. What Blake does claim for the poem is precisely that it is a human artifact, made according to the principles of fallen art at its highest, as Blake conceived them, and no more than this.

What separates art from Eden is the closed gate of Tharmas. When it is finally opened in the awakening of Albion, we pass into paradise in our bodies; and in this passage our bodies are resurrected as the unified, fourfold Albion engaged in the fierce and loving Edenic conversations. Now man has recovered the creative potentialities that in the fallen world were only available to art—and even there in limited form. "Even for the visionary who lives in the divine paradise in which creation and perception are the same

thing," Frye writes, "the gulf between Pygmalion's human
power that conceived a statue and the divine power that
brought it to life still exists." [17] But *Jerusalem* insists on a
modification of Frye's argument, for there no one can find
paradise until all do and the artist is barred from living in
Eden until he has completed his task of universal renewal.
Once the Western Gate of the body is opened, however, the
divine power to create life is exactly what he does possess, if
it is understood that the sense of "he" has undergone a radical metamorphosis: Los is no longer a spectral fragment, but,
as Urthona, has been reintegrated into Albion, to whom, as
a whole, the Edenic creative power is attributed.

In Night IX Blake shows us the difference between fallen
and unfallen imagination, between the labor of art and the
labor of Eden, in one concise and beautiful image:

> Then Tharmas & Urthona rose from the Golden feast satiated
> With Mirth & Joy Urthona limping from his fall on Tharmas
>   leand
> In his right hand his hammer Tharmas held his Shepherds
>   crook. [137: 7–9, E390]

The fallen imagination, as Los, works alone, unsustained by
the full unity and creative power of the body; and in the
same way Tharmas must function apart from the imagination
that could integrate his disorganized faculty. In Generation
we have, through our fallen bodies, a limited capacity to
transform our environment and our lives according to our
desires: the "vegetative body" is the shrunken form of our
constitutive power, our ability to literally make the world.
But the renovation of tongue and touch which completes the
resurrection and gathers the "Parent Power" Tharmas into
Albion makes this ability total. Poetry is directly actualized,
and the source of poetry is no longer the Divine Vision kept
within the fallen imagination, but the body as a whole.

In Blake, the goal of art is the moment at which it be-

comes unnecessary, because the whole of life has taken on
the character of art. Los, poem, and Eden are related to one
another rather as are prophet, prophecy, and actualized
promise in the Old Testament. It is the job of the fallen
artist to reorganize the natural body, to awaken it to its self-
induced limitations and its real potentialities, until it re-
gains the capacity to arise and enter Eden by itself. In this
transformation, what we now recognize as art disappears:
when Albion enters the furnaces, Los drops out of the poem,
consumed with all else in his Sublime Universe. Blake's
point, it seems, is that it is through one of our fallen fragments that the whole can be regathered; not that one particular fragment is, or is to be taken for, or even stands for,
the whole. What Eden is like can be inferred from the experience of artistic work, specifically from those moments in
which the images are entered in imagination; it can be inferred from this, but the two are not, judging from the closing plates of *Jerusalem,* identical; for there, in what seems
to be Blake's most advanced treatment of the theme, we enter
the images in body, in a new life, and together with all other
men.

The Sexes

Another problem raised by the last plates of *Jerusalem*
is the status of sexuality in the risen body. Sexuality occupies
a difficult position in Blake's myth of renovation, and the
Zoa connected with sexual desire, Luvah, is the most com-
plexly ambivalent among Albion's faculties. The problem
is underscored by the special prevalence of sexual concern
in the final chapter of *Jerusalem* and the gradual increase in
tension between spectre and shadow as they approach the
apocalypse: "Albion hath entered the Loins, the place of the
Last Judgment" (J. II: 44: 38, E191).

The difficulty is basically that sexuality, as Blake depicts it, participates in both the given and the desired. In the late work, the words "sex," "nature," and "death" are usually synonymous; and an increasing share of his prophetic outrage is reserved for the sexual temptations of Enitharmon and Vala. At the same time, regeneration always remains an "improvement of sensual enjoyment." The furious opposition to the hypocrisies and the psychic destructiveness of sexual repression is never abated, and the spirit of the *Visions of the Daughters of Albion* survives in full force in the late *The Everlasting Gospel.* To maintain a concept of the late Blake as turning away from the body, one must simply ignore such passages as the following:

> That they may call a shame & Sin
> Loves temple that God dwelleth in
> And hide in secret hidden Shrine
> The Naked Human form divine
> And render that a Lawless thing
> On which the Soul Expands its wing.   [E513]

By the time of *Jerusalem,* Blake is well past the vision of Orc, convinced now that Oothoon cannot liberate herself by the sheer force of her desire, or by any isolated acts, but must instead be emancipated by Los. Yet the Jesus of the last epic, while identified in his aspect of savior with Los, is still in his crucifixion and resurrection a manifestation of Luvah. His resurrection is a sexual one, and his new divinity consists in his forgiveness of the acts of man's body, as well as his refusal to submit to a restricted expression of desire, to a ritual of postponement and secrecy, and to the trappings of sin and guilt which deify the virginity of the Daughters of Albion: "If you dare rend their Veil with your Spear; you are healed of Love!" (J. III: 68: 42, E220).

It would seem from the descriptions of the fall of Tharmas in *The Four Zoas* and that of Albion in *Jerusalem* that the ambivalence is inherent in the nature of the sex act itself, for the total sexual experience in each case is one of division. In intercourse the human form and its emanation are split as masculine and feminine sexual partners; but in this case sexuality is not a joining of two distinct natural bodies, but, rather, a schism of the Edenic integrity into two sexually joined bodies. The emanation is finally severed into a separate place, or other body, in the post-coital separation. I will continue the discussion of the original fall in the final section; what is important here is that the loins are established as the place of externalization, the place of the seed of the masculine and the natural birth of the feminine. Thus, images such as that of Albion at Luvah's Gate, "Leaning against the pillars, & his disease rose from his skirts" (J. II: 46: 1, E193), and that of his Affections appearing outside him as his sons, rending a way in his loins and then "ravning to gormandize / The Human majesty" (J. I: 19: 23–24; E162), do not refer to any particular sexual malady, but, on the contrary, to Albion's complete natural health.[18] His disease and the channel of externalization rent in his body, so injuriously that his Giant Beauty is stretched upon the ground in pain and tears, are figures of a specifically reproduction-oriented sexuality. Because of his emphasis on reproduction as a process of naturalization, Blake can answer the primitivists and the deists, with no imputation whatsoever of original sin, that "man is born a Spectre or Satan & is altogether an Evil" (J. II: 52, E198), for the key word here is "born." The natural child is a "vegetated Spectre," and in Blake birth is a cause for mourning because it is an entry into the Body of Death. In addition, reproduction carries with it the aura of meaningless, self-enclosed, and compulsive repetition that characterizes nature as a whole. The fallen world is a "Sexual Machine" (39: 25, E185); and Los says: "I hear the screech of Childbirth loud pealing, & the groans / Of Death" (30: 23–24, E175).

Blake understands the binding of sexual energy to natural

purposes as a limitation of sexuality to the genitals: "Luvah tore forth from Albions Loins, in fibrous veins, in rivers / Of blood over Europe: a Vegetating Root in grinding pain" (J. II: 47: 4–5, E194). Exiled as a natural seed, the full human energy is imprisoned within a body in which a small part of its range is permitted a fulfillment necessary to the perpetuation of the spectral universe. The remainder of that energy consumes itself and others in the joys of war and destruction, which, the image suggests, replace sensual enjoyment. The following stanza is charged with an intentional and grotesque satire upon the entire social, political, religious, and bodily organization of natural man:

> Albions Spectre from his Loins
> Tore forth in all the pomp of War!
> Satan his name: in flames of fire
> He stretch'd his Druid Pillars far.   [J. II: 27: 37–40, E171]

The natural man as a whole is reduced to the form of a phallus: Albion has become "a little Grovelling root outside himself." And in the following lines, culminating in two of his richest images, Blake's complete myth seems to resonate from the natural organization of the male and female bodies and the mode of genital sexuality:

> Hence the Infernal Veil grows in the disobedient Female:
> Which Jesus rends & the whole Druid Law removes away
> From the Inner Sanctuary: a False Holiness hid within the Center,
> For the Sanctuary of Eden. is in the Camp: in the Outline,
> In the Circumference: & every Minute Particular is Holy:
> Embraces are Cominglings: from the Head even to the Feet;
> And not a pompous High Priest entering by a Secret Place.
>   [J. III: 69: 38–44, E221]

The centralization of sexuality is, like any other centralization in Blake, a tyranny. And not only is our energy limited to this extent, but the sexual center is for us a secret, hidden place with natural veils and moral restrictions militating against fulfillment. In an added touch, the Spectre of Urthona intensifies the shrinkings of Los and Enitharmon, not only by making the social route to sexual fulfillment devious and self-contradictory, but also by encouraging an emotional ambiguity toward the sexual center itself, making it offensive to the sense of beauty, in its Urizenic reduction as the sense of purity:

> The Man who respects Woman shall be despised by Woman
> And deadly cunning & mean abjectness only, shall enjoy them
> For I will make their places of joy & love, excrementitious.
>
> [J. IV: 88: 37–39, E245]

Blake's idea of genital tyranny might be misconstrued to suggest, by way of emancipation, the technique of *coitus interruptus* or a return to the specific "polymorphous perversity" of the child; [19] but what seems clear in other phases of Blake's imagery, that it is the centralization and not the centralized entity—the tyranny of the separated eye and reason, not eye and reason themselves—that he objects to, should be of help here. The point is that the comminglings —which, as Bloom notes, Blake probably bases on Milton's description of angelic sexuality [20]—suggest that the sense of touch will be improved to the extent that the entire body will be susceptible of the same pleasure that is at present reserved for the genitals. There is no special method in this, nor any act of will, for it can only come about spontaneously as part of the general renovation and decentralization of man's body.[21] For Blake a great subtlety of the Urizenic organization is that the highest degree of bodily pleasure is attainable only through an act which ultimately serves to restrict bodily pleasure. At the same time, a restraint from genitality has as its consequence an entry into Ulro, for this is to abandon the remaining fragment of a fully human sexuality, of which genitality is the diminished form.

But Blake's myth of the sexes reaches beyond the particularities of sexual experience. The unfallen Albion is androgynous; and Jerusalem laments: "O Vala! Humanity is far above / Sexual organization" (J. IV: 79: 73–74, E233). The tearing apart of man into two sexes is the fundamental duality of his life in nature, and Blake sees in it the separation between art and life, desire and act, imagination and love, perceiver and object-world, and all the other fallen schisms. In addition to centralizing sexual energy, then, genital organization perpetuates and stabilizes the primal division of the emanation through the reproduction of natural children, split from the start as male and female. As we have seen in the case of Tharmas, sexual separation is portrayed as a consequence of solipsism and self-will, and it implies mortality, as does any sundering of part from whole:

> The Feminine separates from the Masculine & both from Man,
> Ceasing to be His Emanations, Life to Themselves assuming!
>
> . . . . .
>
> When the Individual appropriates Universality
> He divides into Male & Female: & when the Male & Female,
> Appropriate Individuality, they become an Eternal Death.
>   [J. IV: 90: 1–2, 52–54, E247]

Note that Blake distinguishes male and female, on the one hand, from man, or humanity, on the other: all sexual being is inevitably fragmented. In "To Tirzah," Blake tells us that "The Sexes sprung from Shame and Pride" (E30). The creation of two sexes is inherent in the shock of a primal objectification and, more, in any act of fearful or narcissistic self-reflection; sexual differentiation is a direct materialization of the sense of self.

Blake calls the relationship between the disconnected parts "sexual strife." As soon as Enitharmon separates from the loins of Los, his agony subtly modulates into longing, and the

two are consumed by the impossible ambivalences of love
and jealousy, "terrified at each others beauty / Envying each
other yet desiring, in all devouring Love" (J. IV: 86: 63–64,
E243). Los and Enitharmon are Blake's Adam and Eve, and
they are also the first natural children, the embodiments, or
creative accomplishments, of Tharmas' withdrawal from Enion. In *The Four Zoas* Blake gives us in the story of their
growth his fullest exploration of the sexual development of
fallen man. Enion bears the children in the infernal landscape in which the schism has abandoned her: "with fierce
pain she brought forth on the rocks her sorrow & woe / Behold two little Infants wept upon the desolate wind" (I: 8:
1–2, E300). The place of birth is thus established as Ulro.
Blake confirms this in *Jerusalem:* "Such is the nature of the
Ulro: that whatever enters: / Becomes Sexual, & is Created,
and Vegetated, and Born" (J. II: 39: 21–22, E184).

The children wander away from their mother, who pursues
them with "pangs of maternal love," giving them "all her
spectrous life." It seems they would be "repelled" by her
"Into Non Entity revolving round in dark despair" (F.Z. I:
9: 6, E300). But Eno, a "daughter of Beulah," creates for the
lost children Lower Beulah, where the fierce maternity of
Ulro is replaced by a gentle and protective one and the ethos
of Innocence serves as a refuge from natural conflict, given
to the split masculine and feminine until they are sexually
able to enter Generation.

The body of Innocence is pregenital, or perhaps prepubes-
cent. But genitality is implicit in it, and in this sense the
child's body is a seed, an infant desire eventually to be fulfilled in act. Redeemed, the environment of Innocence is
kindly because it encourages the seed to its maturation:

> Where Sexes wander in dreams of bliss among the Emanations
> Where the Masculine & Feminine are nurs'd into Youth &
>   Maiden
> By the tears & smiles of Beulahs Daughters till the time of
>   Sleep is past.   [J. IV: 79: 75–77, E233]

From this period of latency, a "dark slumberous bliss," youth and maiden eventually wake to the choice that confronts Thel and must decide whether to fully enter, through genitality, the world of mortality and vanishing; or, as Thel, to retreat and attempt to remain in Beulah. Thel is a wish not acted upon, an infant murdered in the cradle, a seed that attempts to take root in the watery dreams of Beulah, rather than the earth of Generation. That earth is the only means of access from Lower to Upper Beulah. In the case of Los and Enitharmon, however, Upper Beulah is not yet available to fallen man; Los himself will have to make it so.

Their life as children appears idyllic on the surface, but since they are separate forms from the start and the powers of the undivided human are split between them, and since too they incarnate the fatal emotions of their parents, they can only act out the new universal power struggle:

> Alternate Love & Hate his breast; hers Scorn & Jealousy
> In embryon passions. they kiss'd not nor embrac'd for shame
> & fear
> His head beamd light & in his vigorous voice was prophecy
> He could controll the times & seasons, & the days & years
> She could controll the spaces, regions, desart, flood & forest
> But had no power to weave a Veil of covering for her Sins
> She drave the Females all away from Los
> And Los drave all the Males from her away.
>
> [F.Z. I: 9: 24–31, E301]

Even in this state Los retains an instinct toward renewal; it is again a decisive Blakean theme that everything in Albion's unfallen existence survives the fall in diminished form and, consequently, that the apocalypse is a development of potentialities that are with us now. Here, Los asserts their relationship to the fallen immortals and the primal human integrity, while Enitharmon encourages scorn for them and seeks a separate being. Chafing in the bonds of Los, she sings

"a Song of Death! it is a Song of Vala!" Los resists the naturalization Enitharmon prompts, and he violently casts her
away, smiting her upon the earth. She calls down Urizen as
her champion in the wars of male and female, which are also
in the passage the wars of Albion and Luvah for Vala. But
Los has struck and cast away a part of himself, and the injury
he has given arouses a fatal pity and a desire for the emanation, which is sexually consummated. In the following image,
sexual desire itself is an expression of guilt:

> Los saw the wound of his blow he saw he pitied he wept
> Los now repented that he had smitten Enitharmon he felt
>   love
> Arise in all his Veins he threw his arms around her loins
> To heal the wound of his smiting
> They eat the fleshly bread, they drank the nervous wine.
>   [12: 40–44, E303]

Their sexuality is a devouring of secret bread and a consuming of the Human Form; the body of Innocence becomes
a body of flesh and nerves through a mistaken act of reconciliation between the fragments. The marriage that follows
is a mere amalgamation of the split parts, a deadly wedding
of mind and nature in which the prophetic heritage of Urthona is betrayed; and the first consequence is that Los, formerly accused by Urizen as a "visionary of Jesus," can now
only see the Divine Vision in the distance, high above him:
Albion, clothed in Luvah's robes of blood, shines down "on
the misty earth," while, beneath him, Luvah and Vala are
suspended in the bloody sky, "unable to avert their eyes from
one another." Los's nuptial feast is a nightmarish inaugura-
tion of Urizen's reign and a parody of the apocalyptic banquet of Luvah; its spousal songs call not for the Divine
Breath to go forth over the landscape, but for war and blood;
and Urizenic bards compose proverbs of Heaven: "The
Horse is of more value than the Man" (15: 1, E304).

Once the Spectre of Urthona enters the description of Los's relationship to Enitharmon, the force of desire for the separate feminine is generally localized in Los's natural selfhood; and it is the promptings of the Spectre to regard the objectified emanation with a self-consuming and other-consuming hunger that the prophetic aspiration must resist:

> Thou Knowest that the Spectre is in Every Man insane brutish
> Deformd that I am thus a ravening devouring lust continually
> Craving & devouring but my Eyes are always upon thee O lovely
> Delusion & I cannot crave for any thing but thee.
>
> [F.Z. VIIa: 84: 36–39, E352]

In *Jerusalem* the difficult rebellion of Los against the religion of Female Love is pitted against his Spectre's obsession with the fully vegetated and idolized female, Vala. The separate emanation is now a demoness, who embodies society and nature at their most destructive:

> Her hand is a Court of Justice, her Feet: two Armies in Battle
> Storms & Pestilence: in her Locks: & in her Loins Earthquake.
> And Fire. & the Ruin of Cities & Nations & Families & Tongues.   [J. III: 64: 9–11, E213]

The bliss she promises is no longer of Generation, but of Ulro:

> She cries: The Human is but a Worm, & thou O Male: Thou art
> Thyself Female, a Male: a breeder of Seed: a Son & Husband: & Lo.
> The Human Divine is Womans Shadow, a Vapor in the summers heat
> Go assume Papal dignity thou Spectre, thou Male Harlot! Arthur
> Divide into the Kings of Europe in times remote O Woman-born

And Woman-nourishd & Woman-educated & Woman-scorn'd!
[12–17]

Los recognizes in her

The Sexual Death living on accusation of Sin & Judgment
To freeze Love & Innocence into the gold & silver of the
    Merchant
Without Forgiveness of Sin Love is Itself Eternal Death.
[22–24]

But his Spectre draws Vala into his bosom and they become
a dark Hermaphrodite, the assimilation that signals the
triumph of nature and the end of sexuality in the final totali-
tarian body of the Covering Cherub.

Percival puts it well when he writes that the fall into sex
is presented as a descent into chastity.[22] It is clear that as
natural sexuality develops it moves further and further away
from sensory enjoyment and is increasingly dominated by ul-
terior motives. Luvah's energy has left the loins, and Blake
suggests that the joys of fallen sexuality have more to do with
mind, heart, and eye than with the body. Finally, in the
depths of Ulro, the energy that is denied by the forbidding
Druid priests and the virginal Daughters of Albion is released in violence and destruction. The promises, lures, and
postponements of the courtly rite send man off to war to find
a perverse joy, to win the favor of his mistress, and to consume the energy that would otherwise rend the veil. The
aggregate form of the Virgins is the Great Whore Rahab,
whose fulfillment parodies that offered by Jerusalem. Men,
brought to a final deification of her through the dynamics
of denial and accused pleasure, pay for her with their lives,
and their satisfaction is to wholly lose their individual outlines and to be absorbed into her. Rahab is described as

A Religion of Chastity, forming a Commerce to sell Loves,
With Moral Law, an Equal Balance, not going down with
    decision

> Therefore the Male severe & cruel filld with stern Revenge:
> Mutual Hate returns & mutual Deceit & mutual Fear.
>
> [J. III: 69: 34–37, E221]

In the inversion of the angels, Rahab appears pure and holy, while the spontaneity of Jerusalem becomes prostitution. But for Blake the true harlotry is the internally and externally idolized chastity that deflects an infant desire from its growth and achievement and reifies love as a promise, a reward, a compensation, or a merchandise. In its harshest phase, love becomes a murderous and gratuitous usage of the other, in which even the quest for power and the pleasures of sadism seem almost secondary to the mechanical continuation of an absurd complex of habits. Gwendolen, one of the Daughters of Albion, proclaims:

> I have mockd those who refused cruelty & I have admired
> The cruel Warrior. I have refused to give love to Merlin the
> piteous.
> He brings to me the Images of his Love & I reject in chastity
> And turn them out into the streets for Harlots to be food
> To the stern Warrior.
>   . . . . .
> I have destroyd Wandring Reuben who strove to bind my
> Will
> I have stripd off Josephs beautiful integuement for my Be-
> loved,
> The Cruel-one of Albion: to clothe him in gems of my Zone
> I have named him Jehovah of Hosts. Humanity is become
> A weeping Infant in ruind lovely Jerusalems folding Cloud:
> In Heaven Love begets Love! but Fear is the Parent of
> Earthly Love!
> And he who will not bend to Love must be subdud by Fear.
>
> [J. IV: 81, E236]

Considered in isolation, such passages might be misleading, for Blake's point is that the priests of accusation and the virgins of denial are empowered by the male enjoyment of the rites

of Female Love, of the enticements of distance, of the sub-
stitution of purity for beauty as the object of desire, and of
the pleasures of theft, secrecy, and possession. In Vala's chaste
world, man has been desexualized by making sexual desire an
absolute in itself. Fulfillment becomes subtly irrelevant as
feeling, abstracted from the body, is pursued for its own sake,
so that even torment is eroticized. Virgin, priest, and warrior
are Eternal Characters within the naturalized souls of every
man and woman, and their paradise is a world of pure emotion, of relationship without objects. Blake's anti-mysticism is
nowhere clearer than in his critique of fallen sexuality.

In *The Gates of Paradise*, Blake suggests that sexual organization need not follow the development outlined above:

> When weary Man enters his Cave
> He meets his Saviour in the Grave
> Some find a Female Garment there
> And some a Male, woven with care
> Lest the Sexual Garments sweet
> Should grow a devouring Winding sheet.   [E265]

The Sexual Garments of Generation are sweet when love
does not appropriate universality: "The Imagination is not
a State: it is the Human Existence itself / Affection or Love
becomes a State, when divided from Imagination" (M. II: 32:
32–33, E131). To take any State as an end in itself is to enter
Ulro. The idolization of the genitality of the fallen loins, or
the reason of the fallen brain, or the feeling of the fallen
heart, or, for that matter, even the art of the fallen imagination, is a self-denial that closes one's energy into the Druid
forests. But sexual organization, as well as the most apparently inalienable manifestation of our divisions, is also the
primary condition of renewal. Stripped of guilt and of ul-
terior motivation, sexual love points in the direction of
Albion's wholeness, and in this awareness Los makes available to fallen man in Upper Beulah the reality of Oothoon's

vision of the innocent, enlarging, and internally and externally unifying pleasures of fulfillment. Genital consumma-
tion is a shrunken center, and like every center in Blake it
has an expansive inward being; sexual enjoyment is outside
the dimension of the natural body, just as imagination is
outside that of the mental ratio:

> There is a Grain of Sand in Lambeth that Satan cannot find
> Nor can his Watch Fiends find it: tis translucent & has many
>   Angles
> But he who finds it will find Oothoons palace, for within
> Opening into Beulah every angle is a lovely heaven
> But should the Watch Fiends find it, they would call it Sin
> And lay its Heavens & their inhabitants in blood of punish-
>   ment.   [J. II: 37: 15–20, E181]

Here, beneath Earth's central joint, the Shadow of Jerusalem
finds shelter among Erin and the Daughters of Beulah; the
emanation, in this form, is always available to generative
men and women whenever they can free themselves from the
torments of love and jealousy to find their pleasure in the
sense of touch itself. At the close of *Jerusalem* the Body of
Death is awakened to "Life among the Flowers of Beulah,"
for in Upper Beulah it awakes to another awareness of time
and space, another mode of relationship to the other, another
sense than the visual, and another body than that of the
cavern.

Four modes of sexuality can then be distinguished in
Blake, four states of the sense of touch and of Tharmas as
the complete body in its erotic activity: in Ulro, the absten-
tion from touch or the hostile tactility of violence; in Generation, genital sexuality in its reproductory phase, the
channeling of energy into the maintenance of the cyclical
World of Death, and the secrecy, fears, and jealousies which
become the true objects of sexual pleasure and for which,
indeed, sex serves as a pretext; in Beulah, the realized touch

of affection, genital sexuality in its aspect of pleasure, but pleasure entirely free from any conviction of sin; and in Eden, the complete commingling of the risen activity. What Blake shows us as Eden is a community of human forms embracing through their activity. Now tongue and touch are unified and are, together, reintegrated with the other senses with the effect that the risen activity is a kind of speech, an utterance of the whole man. It would appear that the Edenic conversation and the erotic commingling are identical, the transfigured tactility of the reorganized body, now acting as a whole. This is like no sexuality we know, nor any modification of it, for when Albion awakes, Enitharmon vanishes and there are no longer two sexes. There should be no danger of misconstruing Blake to suggest that the delights of mental endeavor are greater than the delights of natural sexuality, for the distinction between the two only obtains in the separation of male and female, or man and nature. In the fallen world, mental endeavors produce "weak visions of time & space," and bodily pleasure is a shadow of what it might be. But in the resurrection, spiritual and sexual are indistinguishable; indeed the risen body subsists in their new identity. In the following description of Edenic intercourse, Blake opposes the stolen joys and secret bread of natural sexuality to a bodily pleasure incomparably greater:

> When in Eternity Man converses with Man they enter
> Into each others Bosom (which are Universes of delight)
> In mutual interchange. and first their Emanations meet
> Surrounded by their Children. if they embrace & comingle
> The Human-Four-fold Forms mingle also in thunders of
>   Intellect
> But if the Emanations mingle not; with storms & agitations
> Of earthquakes & consuming fires they roll apart in fear
> For Man cannot unite with Man but by their Emanations
> Which stand both Male & Female at the Gates of each Hu-
>   manity

Important

> How then can I ever again be united as Man with Man
> While thou my Emanation refusest my Fibres of dominion?
> When Souls mingle & join thro all the Fibres of Brotherhood
> Can there be any secret joy on Earth greater than this?
>
> [IV: 88: 3–15, E244]

This is a difficult passage, and line 11 is capable of supporting contradictory interpretations. Each man might have four gates, for instance, as paradise does, and his emanations might be "both Male & Female," or themselves androgynous. As I understand the lines, however, the suggestion seems to be that each Edenic Humanity emanates what we would consider to be two sexual persons, a male and a female, at its points of communication with other human forms, as if each Edenic being, then, appeared to others as a deeply and radically unified couple.[23]

It is in its creative power, however, that the human body is most strikingly transformed. While the genitally organized natural body creates life in the form of reproduction, the children of the Edenic commingling are the visionary forms that thunder from the tongue. The implication is that the process of reproduction now ceases; like Godwin, Blake imagines an end to the births of Ulro and the cycle of the generations.[24] The creativities of art and nature are reintegrated as the Loom is returned from Enitharmon to Luvah, and man emanates the entire world in which he lives, including, as the passage above shows, his own sexual garments. Such an increase in creativity depends upon a reorganization of the relationship between art and sexuality. The dictum in *The Marriage* that all forms of energy are from the body is relevant at this point, as is the strange Memorable Fancy in which Blake describes the printing house of Hell:

> I was in a Printing house in Hell & saw the method in which knowledge is transmitted from generation to generation.
>
> In the first chamber was a Dragon-Man, clearing away the rubbish from a caves mouth; within, a number of Dragons were hollowing the cave,

In the second chamber was a Viper folding round the rock &
the cave, and others adorning it with gold silver and precious
stones.

In the third chamber was an Eagle with wings and feathers of
air, he caused the inside of the cave to be infinite, around were
numbers of Eagle like men, who built palaces in the immense
cliffs.

In the fourth chamber were Lions of flaming fire raging
around & melting the metals into living fluids.

In the fifth chamber were Unnam'd forms, which cast the
metals into the expanse.

There they were reciev'd by Men who occupied the sixth chamber, and took the forms of books & were arranged in libraries.
[15, E39]

The process begins with the sexual widening of the doors of
perception by the monsters of energy, who renew the senses
by sweeping them clean of habitual and institutionalized restrictions. At this excess, the Viper attempts to bind the
sexual body, to keep it within the natural context and, by
producing all the allurements of a natural existence, to celebrate the sufficiency of sex as an end in itself. In opposition,
the Eagle of imagination, the "portion of Genius" of the
"Proverbs of Hell," rises from the feeling of freedom and
unrestricted possibility that results from the cleansing in the
first chamber. Next, the Lions of prophetic wrath, in accord
with the teachings of Ezekiel in the earlier banquet scene,
resist present ease and gratification and melt down the non-
human beauties of nature into the primal substance of a new
being. The formless fluids are committed to a chamber of the
new and the unknown, whose workers, themselves nameless,
or unformed, cast them into the human world, where, received by men, as the Prolific imagination by the Devouring
rational consciousness, they appear as books.[25]

In this account the artistic process begins with an upsurge
of sexual fulfillment and culminates, by means of an enlarged
awareness of bodily pleasure, in a poem. The process can be

read, loosely, as analogous to the making of Eden, in which
the responsibility of man for his life is a kind of poetic work
and the final products are no longer books but realized human lives. In Blake sexual desire is ultimately a desire for a
non-natural paradise; and through the artistic work of Los,
who combines the functions of Eagle, Lion, and Unnamed
Form, the progression from Generation to Upper Beulah to
Eden is gradually accomplished. What the progression depends upon is a rise from genitality, which cannot be called
a sublimation because it is a rise from genital satisfaction and
even seems to be inspired by it. Lawrence, I think, is particularly close to Blake when he describes in *Fantasia of the
Unconscious* a sense of renewal following the individual
"commingling of sex," a new energy and enthusiasm that
stimulates us to "the great purpose of manhood, a passionate
unison in actively making a world. This is a real commingling of many." [26] We should bear in mind, however, that
the naturalistic Lawrence would probably have approved of
Blake's description of Edenic sexuality not as a literal potentiality of the senses but as an allegory of collective work,
thereby reducing the new heaven and earth of *Jerusalem* to
the redeemed nature of *Milton*.

It seems that the total human activity in any State of Being
is simultaneously a sexual and a creative activity; the themes
of sensory improvement, production and reproduction, and
the relationship of male and female always refer to both.
The distinction between art and sexuality is maintained,
however, until the final transformation, when both, as we
know them, drop out; in their place is the commingling of
the risen body, an interplay of faculties with each other and
with the total environment they delineate, in which imagination and sexual love reassume their identity, just as soul and
body or perception and creation. Then the word "body" once
again signifies the "real man" and the "whole man," as well
as "all men"; and the fiery lineaments of a finally gratified

desire are perceived in the tactility of a complete human speech.

The Dialectics of Embodiment

Through the final plate of *Jerusalem* we can see "from afar" the process of paradise and, also, the way in which it can lapse once again into history and nature. There, Blake shows us the members of Albion:

> living going forth & returning wearied
> Into the Planetary lives of Years Months Days & Hours repos-
> ing
> And then Awaking into his Bosom in the Life of Immortality.
> [99: 1–4, E256]

Eternal life consists in a particular rhythm of energy and repose, a cycle parodied by our natural seasons, as the Edenic Man periodically departs from his risen body into the three-fold being of Beulah. But this death is now only a kind of sleep, and different from Albion's in that it is a time of refreshment within the world created in Eden. In Beulah, man becomes male and female, and the mode of his repose apparently includes genitality; but his sexuality is now free from possessiveness, mutually expanding, and truly of the body, rather than the consuming natural heart and the Urizenic mind. This is Blake's description of love in Beulah:

> Where every Female delights to give her maiden to her
>   husband
> The Female searches sea & land for gratifications to the
> Male Genius: who in return clothes her in gems & gold
> And feeds her with the food of Eden. hence all her beauty
>   beams
> She Creates at her will a little moony night & silence
> With Spaces of sweet gardens & a tent of elegant beauty:
> Closed in by a sandy desart & a night of stars shining.
> And a little tender moon & hovering angels on the wing.

And the Male gives a Time & Revolution to her Space
Till the time of love is passed in ever varying delights
For All Things Exist in the Human Imagination.

[J. III: 69: 15–25, E221]

In Eden the emanation is the environment, or community, of the human, and is perceived as the translucency,
clarity, brightness, and fire of Eden:

In Great Eternity, every particular Form gives forth or
   Emanates
Its own peculiar Light, & the Form is the Divine Vision
And the Light is his Garment. This is Jerusalem in every
   Man
A Tent & Tabernacle of Mutual Forgiveness Male & Female
   Clothings.
And Jerusalem is called Liberty among the Children of
   Albion.   [J. III: 54: 1–5, E201]

As man is separated from man by the spectral reasoning
power, or detached selfhood, so, Blake writes, man is ad-
joined to man by his Emanative Portion, which is the affirma-
tion of the humanity and holiness of every perceived form. It
is in this conjoining fire that the Edenic body lives. As a
world in the process of its creation, Jerusalem is a fire within
paradise; and there the sources of light are human, rather
than planetary. As a world achieved and identified, Jerusalem appears outside Eden, surrounding it on all sides, as
Beulah (see M. II: 30: 1–31:7, E128). Here the light appears
to originate in a protective planet, and Beulah is both translucent and a "moony night." It is a garden which the Edenic
Man visits, as the God of Genesis visits his Eden "in the cool
of the day" or as the bridegroom in The Song of Solomon
visits the garden of his beloved. As a pastoral world, it has an
external landscape, just as it also contains animal life; but the
landscape is close and gentle, as are the animals, with whom
man can converse. Beulah is a delightful and necessary re-

laxation of one's total humanity, a "watery delusion" in which those parts of Albion that have temporarily become other—his emanated world and his basic energies, or land-scape and animals—are still within the membership of his intimate dwelling place.

Beulah is created at the request of the emanations, when the human energy of Eden becomes too strong for them. The brotherhood of Eden is not a peaceful kind of unison; it is the exuberant warfare of the creative process, and in its tremendous clashes of contraries, achieved forms are destroyed and new ones undertaken, just as fire constantly destroys its own form: "For if we who are but for a time, & who pass away in winter / Behold these wonders of Eternity we shall consume" (M. II: 30: 26–27, E128). Beulah is given to the emanations as a "Temporal Habitation" in which contraries are equally true and no dispute can ever come. However, in receiving a place of their own where they can sustain themselves, the emanations must come dangerously close to constituting a separate object-world. Herein lies the ambivalence of Beulah. To repose in one's creation is to sunder the unific body into male and female bodies of sexual pleasure. Thus the possibility of Ulro is implicit in the myth of an anti-static, rhythmic paradise that is based on the phases of artistic creation from inspiration to completion. The delights of Beulah can also be perceived in this way:

> Humanity knows not of Sex: wherefore are Sexes in Beulah?
> In Beulah the Female lets down her beautiful Tabernacle;
> Which the Male enters magnificent between her Cherubim:
> And becomes One with her mingling condensing in Self-love
> The Rocky Law of Condemnation & double Generation, &
>   Death.   [J. II: 44: 33–37, E191]

The divisive potentiality of Beulah is actualized when Luvah seizes the province of the sleeping Urizen. That Tharmas and Enion should suffer their division as a result of this displacement is inevitable, for the sexual experience of a divided man will itself be divided; Blake intimates that there is no pleasurable experience available to fallen man that is not at a deep level schismatic. It is also inevitable that Tharmas should be the first of the Zoas to be affected: as the sense of touch, he is the medium through which the desire of Luvah must be enacted; as the coherence of the body, any internal disconnection among the faculties must automatically obviate his own power; and as the Lamb of God, the shepherd of Beulah who assures the innocence of our instincts and pleasures, the collapse of spontaneity into a sense of evil must first be felt in his particular domain. Furthermore, when the sexual force of Luvah rushes into the brain, sexual experience is replaced by reasoning about sexual experience, and Tharmas, as the principle of action and mobility, is consumed by a misplaced intellection.[27]

Blake never tells us why it is that the dismemberment of Albion and his massive externalizations, or repressions, begin in Luvah, nor why it is that Urizen has fallen asleep. We might see in the myth of a primal sexual upheaval the revelation of a tyrannical impulse within the sex urge; but this, simply by itself, would ignore too much in the Blakean context of the myth. We might also see in the story a warning that the dream of reason produces monsters; but unless we redefined "reason" as the complete science of imagination and "monsters" as the creatures of reason, Rahab and Satan, this would be a deeply anti-Blakean speculation. It is more likely that Blake is trying in this rich and open-ended narrative to give us the feeling not of an absence of reason, but of an abuse of it, perhaps an intoxication with reason, an hypnosis with its own powers, a laxity born of pride, or a self-congratulatory exaggeration of one faculty until it turns into its opposite—watchfulness into somnolence—just as, in the "Proverbs of Hell," "Excess of laughter weeps."

Integrated with the other Zoas, Urizen is the necessary

Devourer, establishing the momentary horizons of fiery form and limiting as well, one might say, the life-span of any creation. He is the Reaper, the harvester of ripeness, and also the Plowman who in the "Proverbs" drives his cart and his plow over the bones of the dead, preparing the fields for fresh growth. He is Blake's Jesus as revolutionary (exactly the role that falls to Orc in nature), a perpetual upsetter of the merely acquired and the no-longer vital. He is death reclaimed by the imagination and integrated into eternity. But when he acts alone, he becomes a solidifier and a blind conservative, who tries to maintain his disembodied boundaries against all changes in circumstance and desire. His tendency toward constant renovation is distorted into a restless progress in the methodology of control and a tormented questing after stasis.

But what is there in particular about Luvah that drives him, of all the Zoas, to the usurpation? If we consider his functions, we find in them a special penchant toward the external. As the faculty of savoring, he is the force of pleasure in what Albion has created; and, as the faculty of desire, he is the force of motivation that impels Albion to the next Eternity. He is thus inherently directed toward something outer, something that the human has already created or has not yet created. The two functions are simultaneous in the renovated man; his enjoyments in Beulah stimulate him back to Eden: the banquet itself is a seedbed, as in Night IX. When Luvah acts alone, however, the outwardness of love becomes an end in itself. The faculty of pleasure and fertilization seeks to keep the form of desire intact, to perpetuate the transient externalizations of Beulah. Man falls in love with his own creation and abandons the labors of Eden in favor of the already accomplished; a single Eternity, or creative act, is universalized.

But the emanation is only "for a time" and needs constantly to be renewed. Jerusalem is available to Albion only

insofar as she is continuously changing, and thus Blake depicts her as a flickering form, never final, never one thing
only—now city, now woman, now light—but always definite
in the moment. As we have noted, she is described in her re-
entry as a translucent form descending out of heaven, just as
in the Revelation the New Jerusalem is always imaged in
her first descent. For Blake this image is especially significant,
since the integrated emanation only exists in a first appearance. To try to keep her in that form is to transmute her into
the enduring idol Vala. Since every desire is unique and specific, the visionary form can only satisfy the desire of a single
moment, and to seize upon one image, appearance, act, or
system as the gratification of all desire is to grant primacy
to an object and to bind all future desires to the pattern of
the first. Thus, if Jerusalem, at any one instant, is allowed
to remain beyond her initial approach, her fiery outline begins to harden into a Devourer. In Eden, she is constantly
manifesting herself anew, always "descending out of heaven."

In the last plates of *Jerusalem* Blake reiterates in epic form
the feeling of an early Notebook lyric:

> He who binds to himself a joy
> Does the winged life destroy
> But he who kisses the joy as it flies
> Lives in eternity's sun rise.   [E461]

At the close of Blake's myth, living in eternity's sunrise is an
exuberent and demanding process of embodiment, founded
in a dynamics of the poetic process, in which every impulse
of the imagination is fulfilled in an act and then cast off.
In this unending dialectic, acts and bodies are like poems,
each one serving its maker for a moment; Man, the fully
risen faculty that does not exist apart from its activity of
emanation, is alone universal.

It follows ultimately that the myth of Albion awaking to
the changes of perpetual renovation is itself subject to the

same process. Blake's poems describe a reality that, while it can have no effective existence beyond our perceptions and representations of it, can also have no single representation— no single myth; instead, we must keep creating and responding to it in new visions. Blake's own career was faithful to that reality, for he was not a writer who let his poetic tales harden into dogma but was concerned from the beginning of his work to the end to develop, strengthen, and refresh his story of a full humanity. Little in his England could have sustained him; but for Blake the possibility was never less than imminent that Albion's embodiment, the delineation of his immediate life, could be his liberty, or Jerusalem.

Notes

Preface

1. E. D. Hirsch, *Innocence and Experience: An Introduction to Blake* (New Haven: Yale University Press, 1964), pp. 4, 10–12, 145, 162.

2. Gaston Bathelard, the first to recognize this, writes that in Blake, "Une energie imaginée passe du potentiel à l'actif. Elle veut constituer les images dans la forme et dans la matière, remplir les formes, animer les matières." *L'Air et les songes: essai sur l'imagination du mouvement* (1943; rpt. Paris: J. Corti, 1962), p. 97.

3. Northrop Frye, *Fearful Symmetry: A Study of William Blake* (1947; rpt. Boston: Beacon, 1962); Peter Fisher, *The Valley of Vision: Blake as Prophet and Revolutionary*, ed. Northrop Frye, University of Toronto Department of English Studies and Texts, No. 9 (Toronto: University of Toronto Press, 1961); Harold Bloom, *Blake's Apocalypse: A Study in Poetic Argument* (Garden City, N.Y.: Doubleday, 1965).

4. J. H. van den Berg, "The Human Body and the Significance of Human Movement," *Philosophy and Phenomenological Research,* 13 (December 1952), 169. Similarly, in the following characteristic formulation, Maurice Merleau-Ponty finds more inevitable conditions in the act of perception than Blake does: "[The object] is given as the infinite sum of an indefinite series of perspectival views in each of which the object is given but in none of which it is given exhaustively. It is not accidental for the object to be given to me in a 'deformed' way from the point of view (place) which I occupy. That is the price of its being 'real.' " "The Primacy of Perception," trans. James M. Edie, in *The Primacy of*

Perception, and Other Essays, by Merleau-Ponty, ed. Edie, Northwestern University Studies in Phenomenology and Existential Philosophy (Evanston, Illinois: Northwestern University Press, 1964), p. 16.

5. Rilke, "Primeval Sound," a prose-fragment quoted in part by M. D. Herter Norton, "Notes," *Sonnets to Orpheus,* trans. Norton (New York: W. W. Norton, 1962), pp. 145–46.

1. Caverned Man

1. Frye's first chapter in *Fearful Symmetry,* pp. 3–30, is an indispensable study of Blake's revolt against Lockean empiricism. Ernest Tuveson, in *The Imagination as a Means of Grace: Locke and the Aesthetics of Romanticism* (Berkeley: University of California Press, 1960), has demonstrated the extent to which Locke, and eighteenth-century thought in general, was intoxicated with the sense of sight and has shown, as well, how deeply the poetic theory of the age was involved with the eye: he quotes Addison: " 'By the pleasures of the imagination, I mean only such pleasures as arise originally from sight' " (p. 96).

2. Lawrence, *Etruscan Places* (1932; rpt. New York: Viking, 1957), p. 58. Reprinted by permission of The Viking Press, Inc. All rights reserved.

3. John Wild, *Existence and the World of Freedom* (Englewood Cliffs, N.J.: Prentice-Hall, 1965), p. 21.

4. For a discussion of the history of this distinction in archaic thought, see Cornelis Anthonie Van Peursen, *Body, Soul, Spirit: A Survey of the Body-Mind Problem,* trans. Hubert H. Hoskins (London: Oxford University Press, 1966), pp. 87–94.

5. Lawrence, *Apocalypse* (New York: Viking, 1969), p. 85. Copyright 1931 by The Estate of D. H. Lawrence, reprinted by permission of The Viking Press. All rights reserved.

6. Lawrence, *Lady Chatterley's Lover* (New York: Grove, 1962), ch. 13, esp. pp. 241–51.

7. Descartes, *Discourse on Method and Meditations,* trans. Lawrence J. Lafleur, The Library of Liberal Arts, No. 89 (New York: The Liberal Arts Press, 1960), p. 91. Copyright © 1960

by The Liberal Arts Press, Inc., reprinted by permission of The Bobbs-Merrill Company, Inc.

8. Eden, Blake's paradise beyond nature, is one of his four States of Being, together with Generation, the world of ordinary fallen experience; Ulro, an inferno of solipsism; and Beulah, a terrestrial paradise of intimacy and freshness. Beulah comprises a lower level, or Innocence (childhood), and an upper, or Organized Innocence (mature pleasure and repose). Useful introductions to the States can be found in Frye, *Fearful Symmetry*, pp. 48–50, and Bloom, *The Visionary Company: A Reading of English Romantic Poetry* (1961; rpt. Ithaca, N.Y.: Cornell University Press, 1971), pp. 20–31.

9. *Fearful Symmetry*, p. 19.

10. Peter Fisher sidesteps the relationship between the senses and the imagination in a similar way by simply emphasizing the latter, when he asserts that perception actively uses but is independent of the senses. And when he writes that a chief means of cleansing perception is not identifying with what already has been observed, he seems to ignore altogether the condition of sensual enjoyment. The refusal of acquired prefiguration is an important factor in Blakean vision, but Fisher does not show how it is more than a purely mental act; in his formulation the process of cognition remains divided. *The Valley of Vision*, pp. 103, 109.

11. Robert Gleckner, "Blake and the Senses," in *Studies in Romanticism*, 5, No. 4 (Autumn 1965), 1–15.

12. Hazard Adams, *William Blake: A Reading of the Shorter Poems* (Seattle: University of Washington Press, 1963), p. 30.

13. Gleckner, e.g., writes: "Diagrammatically, each of man's senses is the point of intersection, or vortex, of two cones, the open ends of the cones continuing into outer (sensory) and inner (imaginative) infinity" (p. 6). Gleckner follows Adams in what Adams himself calls "the dangerous game of creating diagrams for Blake's thought." See Adams, *William Blake*, pp. 29–34.

14. This has been best formulated by Harold Bloom: "Against the supernaturalist, Blake asserts the reality of the body as being all of the soul that the five senses can perceive. Against the natu-

ralist, he asserts the unreality of the merely given body as against
the imaginative body, rising through an increase in sensual fulfillment into a realization of its unfallen potential." "Dialectic
in *The Marriage of Heaven and Hell*," in *English Romantic
Poets: Modern Essays in Criticism*, ed. Meyer H. Abrams (New
York: Oxford University Press, 1960), p. 82; rpt. from *PMLA*, 73
(1958), 501–04.

15. It is indisputable that Blake found much to like in
Boehme and Swedenborg, and perhaps what he liked most was
the definitive mystic theme of a direct apperception of divinity,
what is called in the Bhagavad-Gita "Open vision / Direct and
instant" (trans. Swami Prabhavananda and Christopher Isher-
wood [New York: New American Library, 1954], p. 79). But the
dualism of inner man and outer man that runs through Boehme
and the Gita, as well as Swedenborg, and the mystic theme of the
increase of the spirit through a dissociation from the senses are
from a strict Blakean viewpoint simply affirmations of the cavern.
Swedenborg does explicitly disengage himself from the conventional mystic themes of transcendence, stasis, and asceticism; but
the most typical of his various attitudes toward the body seems
to be that delight in body, senses, and flesh is a symptom of love
of self and world and closes up the interiors to the potential in-
flux of heavenly joy (*Heaven and Its Wonders, and Hell*, trans.
J. C. Ager [New York: Swedenborg Foundation, 1952], p. 336).
Perhaps it can be said that, in general, Blake attempts to revise
the mystical tradition by separating its concept of immanence
from its concepts of dualism and transcendence and by reconsti-
tuting that idea in terms of the body, human art, and society;
but this revision leaves only surface similarities to the mystics.
For valuable—and more favorable—studies of the relationship
between the esoteric tradition and, respectively, Blake and Romanticism in general, see: Morton D. Paley, *Energy and Imagination: A Study of the Development of Blake's Thought* (Oxford: Clarendon, 1970); and Meyer H. Abrams, *Natural Super-
naturalism: Tradition and Revolution in Romantic Literature*
(New York: W. W. Norton, 1971).

16. Erdman, *Blake: Prophet Against Empire* (1954; rev. Garden City, N.Y.: Doubleday, 1969), p. 178.

2. *The Fallen World*

1. Full surveys of the Zoas are readily available in the critical literature, but I include here an additional note of introduction. In each case, the relationship between the Zoa and his bride reveals a particular phase of fallen man's dissatisfaction. The activity of Luvah is a search for sheer pleasure, his energy comprehending desire, affection, beauty, and love; but when he operates apart from the other Zoas, his quest becomes one of a pure and almost frantic self-gratification. Denied fulfillment, he emerges as Orc, the demon of bodily energy. Vala, his shadow, is the world of natural appearances, its beauty and the illusion of its finality, and she is also the sense of otherness in any emotional relationship. When love becomes spectral, the other becomes only a vital instrument of self-fulfillment, but, at the same time, since she is valued now as an external necessity without which the self cannot achieve satisfaction, she is enlarged as an idol and an enchantress. Vala is the outline of our desires projected onto a pedestal outside ourselves and seized, possessed, or worshipped there, while the inner desires continue to go their own way.

Urthona's world comprises our forms and appearances, both those we imagine and intuit and those we actually perceive. His spectre, Los, is the power of human creativity, and his shadow, Enitharmon, the creativity of nature; her works appear to have a necessity and an actuality that Los's do not, and since they seem to be the source, condition, and inspiration of his art, he is seduced into the imitation of nature, which he can never achieve. His frustration is configured in Enitharmon's position as an unapproachable celestial virgin, who controls the mystique of courtly love.

Urizen, cast loose as an abstract sense of order, represents the pattern of the phenomenon, the system of the social organization, and the code of the individual behavior, when the pattern, system, or code itself is endowed with the status of an ultimate reality and is divorced from the particular as the dictator of its possibilities. Although the inquiry of fallen reason is self-enclosed, directed not toward the particular systems it evolves but merely toward the idea of systematization, Ahania, the bride of his energy, is ironically a knowledge inherently external to him, divine or natural wisdom. Like Descartes, Urizen seeks through himself the laws of a perfect objectivity, and his Ahania is unreachable, a single answer or solution, a secret of life fated always to tantalize and elude the seeker.

Tharmas is bodily instinct, which once, Blake tells us, was precisely an instinct to unified activity: the original benevolence of our instincts is imaged in Tharmas' eternal role as a gentle shepherd in the World of Innocence. His fallen protectorate is the uncontrollable ocean, which to Blake represents sheer matter separated from human consciousness. Now the instincts and bodily processes seem powerful, unknown, and potentially dangerous forces; the spectral form of Tharmas is the draconic Covering Cherub that guards Eden against our re-entry. The shadow of Tharmas is Enion, the aged woman of the earth corresponding to the old man of the sea. She is natural creativity in its chthonic, mysteriously underground aspect; and just as the instincts have become unconscious, so has the genesis of the creative work and of our acts in general. The sense of where things come from has departed from direct knowledge, and we live among forms which seem generated by subsurface powers. Action, as furious as Tharmas' efforts might be, no longer has its ultimate source in human consciousness; Enion is the underlying process of our movements in the world, and process now seems to us divine, natural, historical, or unconscious.

2. In *The Prelude*, for example, Wordsworth describes the intensification of the dissecting powers of his mind,

> till, demanding formal *proof*,
> And seeking it in everything, I lost
> All feeling of conviction, and, in fine,
> Sick, wearied out with contrarieties,
> Yielded up moral questions in despair.   [XI: 301–05]

3. R. D. Laing has written of the way in which stealing "presupposes some boundary between self and not-self." *The Divided Self: An Existential Study in Sanity and Madness* (Baltimore: Penguin, 1966), p. 199.

4. The best study of the problem of self-consciousness in Romanticism is Geoffrey H. Hartman, "Romanticism and Anti-Self-Consciousness," in *Beyond Formalism: Literary Essays 1958–1970* (New Haven: Yale University Press, 1970), pp. 298–310.

5. Rousseau, *Emile, or Education*, trans. Barbara Foxley, Everyman's Library (New York: Dutton, 1950), p. 97.

6. Lawrence, *Etruscan Places*, p. 124.

7. Shelley clarifies the distinction further in *The Defence of Poetry:* "But in the intervals of inspiration, and they may be frequent without being durable, a poet becomes a man and is abandoned to the sudden reflux of the influences under which others habitually live." *Shelley's Prose*, ed. David Lee Clark (1954; rev. Albuquerque: The University of New Mexico Press, 1966), p. 296.

8. Erdman discusses Blake's imagery of disease and plague in its specific historical references and political implications. See *Prophet Against Empire*, pp. 56–85.

9. The best treatment of Blake on Druidism is in Fisher, *The Valley of Vision*, ch. 2 et passim.

10. Kathleen Raine, *Blake and Tradition*, Bollingen Series, No. 35, The A. W. Mellon Lectures in the Fine Arts, No. 11 (2 vols. Princeton: Princeton University Press, 1968). See especially, in reference to my section on the center and circumference, Raine's treatment of the center in conjunction with Boehme's concept of the Punctum (II, 151–71).

11. I employ the term perspective both in the sense of its common usage—mental or physical point of view—and as it is used by the Renaissance perspectivists to denote a mathematical system of vision. Sebastian Serlio (1475–1564), for example in his *The Entire Works on Architecture and Perspective*, explains that perspective consists fundamentally in the acceptance of three lines: a base, "from which all things have their beginnings" and by relation to which a field is made uniform and homogeneous; an horizon, which "is in every place wheresoever sight endeth"; and lines of distance, through which appearances are fixed in an orderly separation from the eye, the horizon, and each other. (See Elizabeth Gilmore Holt, ed., *A Documentary History of Art*, II [1947; rpt. Garden City, N.Y.: Doubleday, 1958], 39–40.)

While to study the full cultural context of Blake's myth of

perception is much beyond the scope of this book, it would be misleading not to nod at least in the direction of the very large historical passage to which his study of the natural eye contributes. We know that the perspectival illusion is an acquired one both for the child and for culture. Its actual codification in the theory of art (many of its techniques, such as foreshortening and proportion, were known to the Greeks) involved a desire to represent faithfully a nature that appeared set before the perceiver in three dimensions, and, like the inventions of printing, landscape painting, programmatic empiricism, and Cartesian rationalism, it seems to suggest a dissociation of the self from the field of its experience and, perceptually, of the eye from the other senses. The history of English poetry bears witness that by the eighteenth century the division, beneath the enthusiasm with which it was pursued, had precipitated a deep sensory crisis, for the major poetic innovations of the post-Augustan and Romantic periods are all based upon a struggle against the foreordained limits of the perspectival field, from the impetus of the Sublime toward expansiveness and boundlessness to the radical sensory experiments of Wordsworth, Coleridge, Shelley, and Keats with their deliberate strivings to heal the schism between subject and object. It is to this broad tradition that Blake's myths and poetic devices primarily belong, rather than to the traditions of the occult or Neoplatonism.

12. Lawrence, *Studies in Classic American Literature* (1923; rpt. Garden City, N.Y.: Doubleday, 1953), p. 94. Copyright 1923, 1951 by Frieda Lawrence, copyright © 1961 by The Estate of the late Mrs. Frieda Lawrence, reprinted by permission of The Viking Press, Inc.

13. The passage is reworked in *Jerusalem* (I: 22, E165–66) with Albion, Vala, and Jerusalem as the principals.

14. Rilke, *The Notebooks of Malte Laurids Brigge,* trans. M. D. Herter Norton (1949; rpt. New York: W. W. Norton, 1958), p. 186.

15. Bachelard, *The Poetics of Space,* trans. Marie Jolas (New York: Orion, 1964), p. 174.

16. Rilke's *Duino Elegies* are exceptionally rich in their analysis of the relationship between natural vision and loss:

Wer hat uns also umgedreht, dass wir,
was wir auch tun, in jener Haltung sind
von einem, welcher fortgeht? Wie er auf
dem letzten Hügel, der ihm ganz sein Tal
noch einmal zeigt, sich wendet, anhäht, weilt—,
so leben wir und nehmen immer Abschied.

Who's turned us round like this, so that we always,
do what we may, retain the attitude
of someone who's departing? Just as he,
on the last hill, that shows him all his valley
for the last time, will turn and stop and linger,
we live our lives, for ever taking leave.

["The Eighth Elegy," ll. 70–75]

Trans. J. B. Leishman and Stephen Spender (1939; rpt. New York: W. W. Norton, 1963), pp. 70–71. Copyright 1939 by W. W. Norton & Company, Inc., copyright renewed 1967 by Stephen Spender and J. B. Leishman, reprinted by permission of W. W. Norton & Company, Inc., Insel Verlag, St. John's College, Oxford, Mr. Stephen Spender, and The Hogarth Press.

17. Rousseau, *Emile,* p. 104.

18. Laing, *The Divided Self,* pp. 73–74. It should be understood, however, that Laing is describing schizoid organization, while Blake's psychology is of normalcy.

19. Rilke, *Malte Laurids Brigge,* trans. Norton, p. 69.

20. Part 2: Sonnet 23, *Sonnets to Orpheus,* trans. Norton: "Bang verlangen wir nach einem Halte" (l. 9, pp. 114–15).

21. See Hazard Adams, *Blake and Yeats: The Contrary Vision* (Ithaca, N.Y.: Cornell University Press, 1955), pp. 104–10.

22. For Frye on the vortex, see *Fearful Symmetry,* pp. 350, 384.

23. Herbert Butterfield describes the Cartesian theory, as follows: "Descartes insisted that every fraction of space should be fully occupied all the time by continuous matter—matter which was regarded as infinitely divisible. The particles were supposed to be packed so tightly that one of them could not move without communicating the commotion to the rest. This matter formed whirlpools in the skies, and it was because the planets were

caught each in its own whirlpool that they were carried round like pieces of straw—driven by the matter with which they were in actual contact—and at the same time were kept in their proper places in the sky. It was because they were all similarly caught in a larger whirlpool, which had the sun as its centre, that they (and their particular whirlpools) were carried along, across the sky, so that they described their large orbits around the sun. Gravity itself was the result of these whirlpools of invisible matter which had the effect of sucking things down towards their own centre. . . . In the time of Newton the system of Descartes and the theory of vortices or whirlpools proved to be vulnerable to both mathematical and experimental attack." *The Origins of Modern Science 1300–1800* (1957; rev. New York: The Free Press, 1965), pp. 159–60. Copyright © 1957 by G. Bell & Sons Ltd., reprinted by permission of G. Bell & Sons Ltd. and The Macmillan Publishing Co., Inc.

24. See Frye, *Fearful Symmetry*, pp. 380–403, esp. 383. Milton Percival, in *William Blake's Circle of Destiny* (1938; rpt. New York: Octagon, 1964), p. 70, calls infernal forms antitheses or travesties of Edenic forms.

3. Renovation

1. E. J. Rose discusses Blake's symbolism of the burin in "Circumcision Symbolism in *Jerusalem*," in *Studies in Romanticism*, 8 (1968), 16–25.

2. Percival, *William Blake's Circle of Destiny*, p. 70.

3. "Blake's last act of forgiveness was one that even went beyond [the] merciful reconciliation with the Blake of Experience. In the great, final apocalypse of the poem (plate 98), Blake depicts the redemption of his perennial spiritual enemies, Bacon, Newton, and Locke. They, too, are saved by his now invincible Mercy and Pity, along with Milton, Shakespeare, and Chaucer. The reader familiar with Blake's comments on Bacon, Newton, and Locke will regard this final act of magnanimity with awe." Hirsch, *Innocence and Experience*, pp. 164–65.

4. Fisher, *The Valley of Vision*, pp. 218–19. It should be noted

that Blake also speaks of a State of Rahab, a State of Milton, a State of Adam, and so forth. Any world, body, condition, organization, or viewpoint is understood by Blake as a phase of individual possibility, a particular moment, or station of the mental traveler, in the departure from or approach to unfallen integration.

5. Shelley, for example, in *The Defence of Poetry,* poses the differentiations of autonomous reason against the relationships of the poetic imagination, and the calculations of detached selfhood against the sympathies that go beyond the self: "Thus poetry and the principle of self, of which money is the visible incarnation, are the God and Mammon of the world." (*Shelley's Prose,* p. 293.) Similarly, Blake, in *The Laocoön,* pits art against money, the one expansive body of the imagination against the idol-body of separateness: "Christianity is Art & not Money . . . Money, which is The Great Satan or Reason the Root of Good & Evil In The Accusation of Sin" (E271). And in *A Vision of the Last Judgment* the sun of fallen perception is somewhat like a *guinea.*

6. In Wordsworth, Coleridge, and Shelley, the reintegration typically takes the form of a shattering or ecstatic visitation that transfigures the landscape. Rilke writes of such a moment: "Everywhere appearance and vision came, as it were, together in the object, in every one of them a whole inner world was exhibited, as though an angel, in whom space was included, were blind and looking into himself." (*Briefe aus den Jahren 1914–1921,* quoted in Leishman, "Introduction," *Duino Elegies,* p. 10.) And for Bachelard the appearances of nature are shaped by the reverie of the perceiver: "Dans nos yeux c'est *l'eau* qui rêve." The reverie operates within the appearances, and the phenomenal world is the dreamer. (*L'Eaux et les rêves: essai sur l'imagination de la matière* [Paris: J. Corti, 1942], p. 45.) In a general sense, *Jerusalem* can be regarded as the deep story of the Romantic visionary moment, for it describes how all fallen existence from the creation to the present is involved, as obstacle, in any single act of authentic perception.

7. The relations of Jerusalem and Vala are prefigured in the

symbolism of lewdness that emerges with particular power in two chapters of Ezekiel. In 16, the Lord castigates Jerusalem, who, despised at birth, has been taken as His bride, for forgetting that all her beauties and prosperities are "perfect through my comeliness, which I had put upon thee": "But thou didst trust in thine own beauty, and playedst the harlot because of thy renown, and pouredst out thy fornications on every one that passed by; his it was" (16:15). Taking herself as a source, she has made images of men from the jewels God gave her, and she has sacrificed her children to them. In 23, Aholibah, or Jerusalem, has followed her sister, Aholah, or Samaria, into the whoredoms of idolatry, surpassing her in corruption, and God warns that her lovers—those whose images she has doted upon—will rise up against her. In Blake's poem, with its "infernal" reading of the Bible, the accusation of harlotry against Jerusalem is a false one, although she herself is convinced of its truth. The difference is essentially that in Blake the Lord God becomes the tormented Albion. Blake also follows out the metaphor of harlotry to a vision, absent in Ezekiel's argument, of the sexual roots of idolatry, for Jerusalem is cast out when love becomes sin.

8. Lines 104–05 ("They need not extraordinary calls / To rouse them") would seem to qualify severely the relevance of the passage to Blake; but, beside the fact that these two poets crucially qualify each other at most points of contact, Blake would probably say that the calls he describes are not extraordinary, that they are there for anyone, at any time, to hear.

9. Trans. Leishman and Spender (pp. 76–77). The original German is:

> vergänglich,
> traun sie ein Rettendes uns, den Vergänglichsten, zu.
> Wollen, wir sollen sie ganz im unsichtbarn Herzen verwandeln
> in—o unendlich—in uns! wer wir am Ende auch seien.
>
> Erde, ist es nicht dies, was du willst: unsichtbar
> in uns erstehn?—Ist es dein Traum nicht,
> einmal unsichtbar zu sein?—Erde! unsichtbar!

Was, wenn Verwandlung nicht, ist dein drängender Auftrag?

[65–72]

10. Ibid. (pp. 82–86):

Nicht erfasst es sein Blick, im Frühtod

schwindelnd. Aber ihr Schaun,

hinter dem Pschent-Rand hervor, scheucht es die Eule. Und
sie,

streifend im langsamen Abstrich die Wange entlang,

jene der reifesten Rundung,

zeichnet weich in das neue

Totengehör, über ein doppelt

aufgeschlagenes Blatt, den unbeschreiblichen Umriss.

[81–88]

11. Jean Hagstrum, *William Blake: Poet and Painter: An Introduction to the Illuminated Verse* (Chicago: University of Chicago Press, 1964), pp. 14–15.

12. Quoted in Francis Berry, *Poetry and the Physical Voice* (London: Oxford University Press, 1962), p. 36.

13. I follow Bloom in concentrating on the speaker, rather than the tiger (*Blake's Apocalypse,* pp. 146–48). Morton D. Paley has noted the similarity of the speaker's questions to those of Job, but finds in the similarity an attempt by Blake to evoke (without irony) the terror of the Sublime. "Tyger of Wrath," in Paley, ed., *Twentieth Century Interpretations of the Songs of Innocence and Experience* (Englewood Cliffs, N.J.: Prentice-Hall, 1969).

14. For a discussion of the way in which *The Four Zoas* offers a collision of "contradictory truths" without a context, see Helen T. McNeil, "The Formal Art of *The Four Zoas*," in David V. Erdman and John E. Grant, eds., *Blake's Visionary Forms Dramatic* (Princeton: Princeton University Press, 1970), pp. 373–90. Gleckner, in discussing the *Songs,* has emphasized the vital importance of viewpoint (*The Piper and the Bard: A Study of William Blake* [Detroit: Wayne State University Press, 1959], esp. p. 64); as has Henry Lesnick, in writing of *Jerusalem* ("The Function of Perspective in Blake's *Jerusalem,*" *Bulletin of the New York Public Library,* 73, No. 1 [January 1969], 49–55).

15. Book VI, lines 78–86. *John Milton: Complete Poems and*

Major Prose, ed. Merritt Y. Hughes (New York: Odyssey, 1957), pp. 325–26. Copyright 1957 by The Odyssey Press, Inc., reprinted by permission of The Bobbs-Merrill Company, Inc.

16. Sergei Eisenstein, *The Film Sense,* in *Film Form* and *The Film Sense,* ed. and trans. Jay Leyda (New York: Harcourt, Brace, 1957), pp. 58–62. For an excellent study of the relationship between film and Romantic style in general, see Bloom, "The Visionary Cinema of Romantic Poetry," in Alvin Rosenfeld, ed., *William Blake: Essays for S. Foster Damon* (Providence: Brown University Press, 1969), pp. 18–35.

17. Frye, *Anatomy of Criticism* (Princeton: Princeton University Press, 1957), p. 236.

18. John Hollander, "Blake and the Metrical Contract," in Frederick W. Hilles and Harold Bloom, eds., *From Sensibility to Romanticism: Essays Presented to Frederick A. Pottle* (London: Oxford University Press, 1969), pp. 293–310, esp. 309.

19. Frye, *Anatomy of Criticism,* p. 270.

20. "Blake and the Metrical Contract," p. 308. Damon writes that "Blake does not consciously pass from one species of foot to another; he mingles them at the instantaneous prompting of his ear"; and that his fourteeners are intended to be "poured out in a great flood of oratory, stressing the natural accents, and passing rapidly over the unaccented syllables. Each line represents a breath." *William Blake: His Philosophy and Symbols* (Gloucester, Mass.: Peter Smith, 1958), pp. 47, 57.

21. Francis Berry, *Poetry and the Physical Voice,* p. 193.

22. Fisher emphasizes that music, "as the least naturalistic of the arts," is associated with the imagination (*The Valley of Vision,* p. 241); and critics, particularly Frye and S. Foster Damon, have often compared the stylistic and structural principles of Blake's work, especially in *Jerusalem,* to the dynamics of music. (See Karl Kiralis, "The Theme and Structure of Blake's *Jerusalem,*" in *ELH: A Journal of English Literary History,* 23 [June 1956], 127–43, for a brief summary of pre-1956 accounts of the poem's structure.) In light of the pervasive Romantic impulse to align poetry with music, rather than painting, and in light, also, of the strivings for the effects of music in such later poets as Tennyson, Mallarmé, Swinburne, and Poe, the analogy is

worth keeping in mind. Blake himself, on the other hand, clearly distinguishes poetry, painting, and music, and he tends to think of poetry in conjunction with, not *as*, other art forms—although, as I will suggest in the final chapter, he seems to be looking forward to a universal art medium. But at the level of technique, the complexities of *Jerusalem* remain poetic, rather than symphonic. The musical analogy, as used by Blake's critics, should probably serve as no more than a preliminary excursus to modify the distortions which a visually based critical terminology may exercise on a poem like *Jerusalem*. Judging by the experience of Eliot with Milton, for one example, it would seem that our chief critical approaches are poorly equipped to do justice to an entire tradition of verse that depends upon the ear, or to understand the auditory dimension of a poem as anything more than its sound. George Whalley, commenting on the role of the ear in poetry of all types, suggests that such words as "resonance," "reverberation," and others of his own devising would indicate better than the prevailing terms the crucial elements of time, rhythm, and recurrence in the "image." (See *Poetic Process: An Essay in Poetics* [Cleveland: World, 1967], esp. pp. 161–63.) The issue is a rich and multifaceted one. The possibility explored in the present chapter is that for Blake voice and speech constitute a peculiar sensory realm of their own.

23. This sensory complexity, of course, is greatly intensified in Blake's illuminated page (especially since his anti-naturalistic graphic style, by itself, works against the given eye), but I am restricting myself to effects that are present in Blake's words even when they are reprinted apart from their original setting. The strife assumes added proportions when we regard it from such a context as that outlined by the phenomenologist Georges Gusdorf: "The invention of writing overthrew the first human world and permitted the development of a new mental age. . . . Speech had given to man domination of his immediate space. But, bound to the concrete present, it can attain in scope and duration only an horizon limited to the fleeting boundaries of consciousness. Writing permits the separation of the voice from the present reality and thereby expands its range. Writings remain, and by that means they have the power to fix the world, to

stabilize it in duration. Likewise, they crystallize and give form to a personality which then becomes capable of signing his name and of making himself felt beyond his bodily limits. Writing consolidates speech." (*Speaking* [*La Parole*], trans. Paul T. Brockelman, Northwestern University Studies in Phenomenology and Existential Philosophy [Evanston, Illinois: Northwestern University Press, 1965], p. 111.) Blake might revise the description to suggest that speech returns the fleeting boundaries of consciousness to writing. It should also be noted that in McLuhanist terms Blake is richly inconsistent, with his love of organic "Gothic" form and his equal love of Renaissance poetry, art, and media.

24. Mailer's mythology of smell is most extensively worked out in *An American Dream* and *Why Are We in Vietnam?* Related, in a strange way, to his usage is Swedenborg's version of the improved sense of smell, which, among his angels, assumes a far-reaching cognitive capacity, as it has in animals: the angels can identify the state of being of an approaching individual by his odor before he enters their visual range (*Arcana Coelestia,* V [New York: American Swedenborg Printing and Publishing Society, 1873], 258–60). A powerful example of the Proustian tradition occurs in Wallace Stegner's *Wolf Willow* (New York: copyright © 1962 by Wallace Stegner, reprinted by permission of The Viking Press, Inc.), in which the author, returning to a childhood home after a long absence, is unable to "re-establish . . . an ancient, unbearable recognition" of the changed setting, until he comes upon its characteristic odor, the "wholly native smell" of wolf willow. Then all at once, "the queer adult compulsion to return to one's beginnings is assuaged" (pp. 18–19).

25. Van den Berg's theory of the body as constituted, in one of its phases, by the loving and encouraging glance of the other, is suggestive here. "The Human Body," *Philosophy and Phenomenological Research* 13 (December 1952), 175, 181–82.

26. Swedenborg, too, tells us of four types of vision: (1) the sight of dreams, when the natural eyes are closed in sleep; (2) natural sight, when the eyes of understanding are completely closed; (3) the sight when the eyes of understanding are open, and we see representations from heaven but rather obscurely

and "differing entirely from the common imagination of men";
and (4) most exquisite of all, pure spiritual sight, when man is
in spirit separated from his body. (*The Spiritual Diary*, trans.
J. H. Smithson, I [New York: L. C. Bush, 1850], 178.) But the
idea of closing the eye to see better was satirized early by Blake
in the character of Obtuse Angle in *An Island in the Moon*.
Swedenborg's spiritual sight, taking us utterly outside the sensory things that make up the sphere of the eye's potential redemption, would be merely another variety of Ulro vision.

27. *Treatise on Painting,* quoted in Merleau-Ponty, "Eye and
Mind," trans. Carleton Dallery, in *The Primacy of Perception,*
p. 183.

28. "Eye and Mind," p. 184.

29. Hartman, *The Unmediated Vision: An Interpretation of
Wordsworth, Hopkins, Rilke, and Valéry* (1954; rpt. New York:
Harcourt, Brace & World, 1966), p. 91. Lawrence's observations
on Etruscan painting are interesting here, although he finds the
word "outline" unacceptable. "The subtlety of Etruscan painting, as of Chinese and Hindu, lies in the wonderfully suggestive
edge of the figures. It is not outlined. It is not what we call
'drawing.' It is the flowing contour where the body suddenly
leaves off, upon the atmosphere. The Etruscan artist seems to
have seen living things surging from their own centre to their
own surface . . . It must have been a wonderful world, that old
world where everything appeared alive and shining in the dusk
of contact with all things, not merely as an isolated individual
thing played upon by daylight; where each thing had a clear outline, visually, but in its very clarity was related emotionally or
vitally to strange other things, one thing springing from another,
things mentally contradictory fusing together emotionally, so
that a lion could be at the same moment also a goat, and not a
goat." *Etruscan Places,* pp. 112–13.

30. Now obsolete meanings of the word "taste" include "to
feel, to handle" and, still used in the eighteenth century, "to
have carnal knowledge of" (*O.E.D.*).

31. *Apocalypse,* p. 42.

32. See Richard Harter Fogle: "The synaesthetic imagery of
Keats is almost always actuated by a desire to attain the fullest

possible sensuous effect. It frequently appears as a tendency to ally sense-images with the sense of touch in order to make them stronger and more concrete." *The Imagery of Keats and Shelley* (1949; rpt. Hamden, Connecticut: Archon, 1962), p. 106.

33. Lawrence, *Etruscan Places*, p. 78.

4. *The Body of Imagination*

1. *Heaven and Hell*, p. 399.

2. Ibid., p. 126.

3. Ibid., pp. 399–400.

4. See 133: 14–15; and 138: 15, E391.

5. It is worth noting that Albion's awakening still involves political upheaval: he rises "in direful / Revolutions of Action & Passion" (IV: 95: 9–10, E252).

6. Ernest Tuveson, *Imagination as a Means of Grace*, p. 73.

7. "The Film and the New Psychology," in *Sense and Non-Sense*, by Maurice Merleau-Ponty, trans. Hubert L. Dreyfus and Patricia Allen Dreyfus, Northwestern University Studies in Phenomenology and Existential Philosophy (Evanston, Illinois: Northwestern University Press, 1964), pp. 49–50.

8. Relevant, as well, is the fourfold body described by Lawrence in his attempt to return consciousness and the body to each other. The "coming to perfection of each single individual" depends upon a dynamic interchange among the four poles of "the first, basic field of consciousness" (which are located in the solar plexus, lumbar ganglion, cardiac plexus, and thoracic ganglion) and a "passionate flux" among their various sympathetic and separatist currents. See his two responses to Freud, *Psychoanalysis and the Unconscious* and *Fantasia of the Unconscious* (New York: Viking, 1960), p. 41 et passim. Copyright 1921 and 1922 by Thomas B. Seltzer, Inc., renewed 1949 and 1950 by Frieda Lawrence, reprinted by permission of The Viking Press, Inc.

9. Percival accounts for the surprising use of the name Jehovah as signifying the imagination as an "outward image" in Eden (*William Blake's Circle of Destiny*, p. 142). But Blake's chief intention, one would think, would be to indicate Albion's

replacement of the position occupied at present by Jehovah, the re-establishment of renovated man as the creator of his own universe. What the name signifies is that there is no other Jehovah.

10. J. H. van den Berg, *The Changing Nature of Man: Introduction to a Historical Psychology*, trans. H. F. Croes (New York: Dell, 1964), p. 198.

11. Frye, *Fearful Symmetry*, p. 138.

12. Merleau-Ponty, "Eye and Mind," in *The Primacy of Perception*, p. 189.

13. Frye, *Fearful Symmetry*, p. 89.

14. Ibid., p. 91.

15. In general, the Blake criticism most advanced in these areas tends to blur the distinction in the same way that Frye does. Bloom comes closest to keeping the relationship clear but can still identify Golgonooza as "the New Jerusalem or City of Eden," even while, in the same passage, he correctly likens it to Spenser's Cleopolis. *The Visionary Company*, p. 111.

16. Adams, *Blake and Yeats*, pp. 104, 109; Kiralis, "The Theme and Structure of Blake's *Jerusalem*," *ELH*, 23 (June 1956), 142.

17. Frye, *Fearful Symmetry*, p. 280.

18. Contrast Bloom, "Commentary," in *The Poetry and Prose of Blake*, p. 849.

19. Contrast N. O. Brown's pairing of Blake and Bosch in *Love's Body* (New York: Random House, 1965), p. 137. Brown valuably notes the importance and the basic implications of Blake's sexual imagery and also advances our awareness of the body in late Blake, but the connection with polymorphous perversity is not a Blakean one, as Brown formulates it. Unlike Wordsworth, Blake is opposed to even a provisional return to an earlier stage of natural development, and the polymorphous sexuality which Albion reassumes is one outside the capacity of either the mature or the infantile fallen body.

20. Bloom, *Blake's Apocalypse*, pp. 456–57.

21. Naturalistic analogues to this structure of decentralization can be found in Lawrence and Wordsworth, both of whom portray a delocalization of energy from a single point of fixation over the environment as a whole. *Sons and Lovers* (New York: Viking Press, 1958), for instance, ends with a transposition of

radiance from Paul Morel's mother to the world of mature possibility. Paul feels that, with his mother's death, "Life ahead looked dead, as if the glow were gone out." Drawn to follow her into the "immense dark silence," he finally turns "towards the city's gold phosphorescence." For Wordsworth, all things were once "Apparelled in celestial light" ("Ode: Intimations of Immortality"), a radiance lost when the "light of sense" is centralized in the mature eye. But, as with Blake's translucence, the departed splendor remains within the landscape, locked into Spots of Time, powerhouses of imaginative and, in the largest sense, erotic energy, which can be tapped to infuse the entire relationship of the poet with the natural world.

22. Percival, *William Blake's Circle of Destiny*, p. 117.

23. Blake leaves the mythic potentialities of this image undeveloped, and there are, I believe, no exact parallels elsewhere in his writings to help us. There might be some sense at this point in a limited comparison with Swedenborg and Boehme, both of whom use a sexual imagery for the completion of the risen man. Swedenborg's angelic being is figured as a married couple, a theme excellently developed by Balzac in the title character of *Seraphita,* who before resurrection appears as a man to women and a woman to men, rising finally as a wedded pair. For Boehme, the desire we interpret as sexual actually aims for a total human completion, as the female, or body, desires a celestial heart, and the male, or head and soul, a corporeal matrix: "And thus the vehement desire in the Feminine and Masculine Gender of all Creatures doth arise, so that one longeth after the other for copulation" (*The High and Deep Searching of the Threefold Life of Man,* ix: 114, in *The Works of Jacob Behmen,* trans. William Law, 4 vols. [London: M. Richardson, 1764–81], II, 100). Physical sex itself is another matter, however, and both writers tend merely to excuse it. "The delight of marriage, which is a purer and more exquisite delight of touch, transcends all the rest because of its use, which is the procreation of the human race and therefore of angels of heaven" (*Heaven and Hell,* p. 344). Boehme's attitude toward natural sexuality seems at times one of sheer revulsion: "Therefore, O Man, look to it! (have a care) how you use the bestial Lust; it is (in itself) an Abomina-

tion before God, whether it be in the State of Wedlock, or outside of it. But the right Love and Fidelity (in the Fear of God)
covers it before the Countenance of God; and (through the Sun
of the Virgin) it is regenerated to be a pure undefiled Creature
again, in the Faith, if thy Confidence be in God" (*The Three
Principles of the Divine Essence*, xx: 56, in *Works*, I, 207).

24. Godwin, *Enquiry Concerning Political Justice and Its In-
fluence on Morals and Happiness*, ed. F. E. L. Priestley, University of Toronto Department of English Studies and Texts, No. 2,
3 vols. (Toronto: University of Toronto Press, 1946), II, 528.

25. I am interpreting the Printing Press of Hell in its relevance to the matters under discussion, but the sequence can be
taken on many levels and no single paraphrase is in itself adequate to its fantasy. In reading the passage on any level, the
crux, to my mind, is whether the Viper is presented in a favorable or unfavorable light. I am inclined to agree with Bloom
("Commentary," p. 812) in finding the latter more likely, although I take the Viper to be not so much an emblem simply of
"restraint and custom" as an emblem of generative sexuality,
the serpentine Orc with its double nature, at once monstrous to
the angel in man and subtly restrictive to the devil.

26. Lawrence continues that "no great purposive passion can
endure long unless it is established upon the fulfillment in the
vast majority of individuals of the true sexual passion." (See
Fantasia, pp. 144–45). In this essay, Lawrence opposes a male
(religious, creative) motive to a female (sexual); but without a
corresponding myth of the original or radical androgyny of
every natural being, he is forced to see man and woman as the
literal embodiments of these impulses and thus to envision a
"great unison of manhood" (p. 144), rather than, as Blake does,
a unison of mankind.

27. The doubts, analyses, and inquisitions of Tharmas are
illuminated by Lawrence's condemnations of the conceptuali-
zation or idealization of sex, and of life in general: "we live from
the head"; "The passions or desires which are thought-born are
deadly"; "[The modern] child does not so much want to *act* as
to *know*." *Fantasia*, pp. 118–19, 121, 155.

Index

The Awakening of Albion

Designed by R. E. Rosenbaum.
Composed by Vail-Ballou Press, Inc.,
in 11 point linotype Baskerville, 2 points leaded,
with display lines in A.T.F. Baskerville.
Printed letterpress from type by Vail-Ballou Press
on Warren's 1854 Regular, 60 pound basis,
with the Cornell University Press watermark.
Bound by Vail-Ballou Press
in Columbia book cloth
and stamped in All Purpose foil.